PhilanthropyRoundtable

Closing America's High-achievement Gap

A Wise Giver's Guide to Helping Our Most Talented Students Reach Their Full Potential

Andy Smarick

Karl Zinsmeister, series editor

Current and Upcoming Wise Giver's Guides from The Philanthropy Roundtable

Karl Zinsmeister, *series editor*

For all current and future titles, visit PhilanthropyRoundtable.org/guidebook

TABLE OF CONTENTS

PREFACE

Mediocrity at the top

When K-12 education philanthropists consider underserved students, they conjure up an image of low-income, urban children trapped in a wasteland of poor schools. While there is much truth in this, another category of underserved students exists in this country. These children possess the potential to be our greatest thinkers, scientists, artists, teachers and leaders—they are our high-potential students, sometimes referred to as "gifted."

For decades, philanthropists have striven to raise academic outcomes for our lowest-performing students, and significant progress in closing the "achievement gap" has been made. This guidebook by Andy Smarick lays out a compelling case for why funders should also address another gap: the "high-achievement gap" separating the U.S. from competing nations.

Of the 60 million or so American school children, how many are quick learners who are never challenged to their full potential? How many students of every economic, ethnic, and geographic group will languish in school not because it is too difficult or they lack drive, but because the paltry academic options they are afforded fail to stretch or challenge them?

The donors profiled in this guidebook show that philanthropy can dramatically enhance the learning level of high-potential students, including those from low-income families. This work can be taken up on its own, or woven seamlessly into broader education support. But if ambitious and passionate donors fail to make this issue a priority, it is likely to remain one of the great failings of the U.S. education system for decades to come, penalizing many children and the nation as a whole.

If you would like to enter a network of hundreds of top donors from across the country who debate strategies and share lessons learned, we hope you will consider joining The Philanthropy Roundtable. We offer intellectually challenging and solicitation-free meetings, customized resources, consulting, and private seminars for our members, all at no charge.

For more information, please contact any of us: (202) 822-8333 or K-12@PhilanthropyRoundtable.org.

Adam Meyerson
President
The Philanthropy Roundtable

Dan Fishman, Director
Anthony Pienta, Deputy Director
K–12 education programs

INTRODUCTION

There is something quintessentially American about beating the odds, bootstrapping your way to success.

That is the story of waves of immigrants who came to our shores and made their marks. It's the tale of the hardy souls who crossed the plains and mountains to realize their destinies and the nation's. It's the heart of the American Dream—the innumerable impoverished but steel-willed young people who studied hard, got jobs or started businesses, saved for their first homes, scraped and worked and ultimately achieved things that once seemed far beyond reach.

A related strand in our national consciousness is our slight disdain—maybe better described as a collective chip on our shoulder—for those seen as undeservingly privileged. Ours is the country of "We the people," a humble nation that cast off the crown, all nobility, and the haughty pretentions that go along with class privilege. We rebel against not just tyranny but also the overarching Platonic idea of "philosopher kings"—persons groomed from youth, told they are crafted from precious metals, and guided into positions of power and lives of advantage. That is the system our forefathers left the old country to get away from.

We think proudly of our greats who made it big despite strong odds against them. Frederick Douglass, once a slave, becomes a national leader. Rising above rural poverty, less than a year of schooling, homeliness, and depression, Abraham Lincoln turns into a nation saver. Steve Jobs, given up for adoption and then a college dropout, ends up one of the most productive Americans ever.

Thomas Edison, who was self-taught from the age of seven, gave a particularly American flair to these self-invention stories with his famous maxim that "Genius is 1 percent inspiration, 99 percent perspiration." It seems that we, as a nation, *respect* what people become, but we reserve our *reverence* for the process of rising—the stark *becoming*.

This tension casts a shadow over the education of quick learners in America.

We have the proudest tradition of accessible schooling in the world. Much earlier than other nations, our "common" public schools offered a free education to all. Catholic and other religious schools have provided instruction to the disadvantaged since before America's founding. The charter schools that are now the focus of so much special effort and philanthropic spending are predominantly oriented toward the most underserved boys and girls in our inner cities.

As a nation, we have recognized from the beginning that an education is essential to "the becoming." Our tuition-free schools, our numerous programs for low-income and special-needs children, the many educational gifts of donors, and much more are explained by this. We seek to continue this strain of fundamentally democratic, egalitarian support for young climbers, through schools that will help them arrive no matter how humble their starting points.

But for one group of students, we seem to hedge: those with special mental gifts, those deemed high-potential, those achieving at an unusually advanced level. Perhaps this is caused by our instinctive aversion to privilege. These students were blessed, they were given capacity and talent to spare. "They did nothing to deserve this," whispers the undercurrent. "They were endowed with unusual intelligence by good fortune, and are likely to accumulate interest in the future."

We certainly have no intention of holding back our top students. But just as surely we are inclined to let them be. They will be fine without any favors from us, goes the thinking.

As a result, for kids having trouble in school we now have aggressive philanthropic interventions of all sorts, Title I spending and Pell Grants, networks of high-poverty charter schools, "equity lawsuits" and the Individuals with Disabilities Education Act, and countless scholarship programs for the low-income. All efforts we can be enormously proud of.

But for our intellectually gifted students (many of whom are far from "privileged" economically, emotionally, or otherwise, truth be told) we have an astonishingly under-resourced, deprioritized, and inchoate system of school supports. Guiding children to the very

> For our intellectually gifted students (many of whom are far from "privileged" economically, emotionally, or otherwise, truth be told) we have an astonishingly weak system.

highest levels of academic achievement falls low on the priority list of most schools today, far below equity, diversity, and extracurriculars. Were Plato with us today, he might scold us with a warning that "By not cultivating excellence, you are dishonoring it."

Not only is this tragic for many students, it flies in the face of national realities. The truth is, many of the most admired *becomers* from our past were talented people who were given special help along the way. Douglass received surreptitious reading lessons during his childhood. Edison was home-schooled by an attentive mother. Robert Goddard was given a telescope, microscope, and subscription to *Scientific American* during formative years. Steve Jobs was encouraged and aided in following his unconventional fascination with technology.

These and other nation-changers didn't just luck into their destinies. They made them through countless hours of reading, study, experimentation, and code-writing—usually fostered and assisted by sponsors who noticed their gifts and took measures to exercise and deepen them. Many of America's greatest contributions were made by boys and girls who combined innate capacities with internal grit and external encouragement to make great things happen.

This book never argues for a moment that less attention should be given to America's most at-risk kids. Instead, it argues that we ought to give increased attention to those at the top—both for their own sake and for the nation's. And we believe strongly that philanthropists can lead the way in showing that these are not mutually exclusive undertakings.

In the pages to come, we make the case for why gifted education is important and why it should matter to donors. Then we provide general history and other background information on this unfortunately nebulous field so funders are able to see it in the context of education reform more generally and their current giving strategies. The bulk of the book is then dedicated to the various strategies and tactics a philanthropist might employ to support education of high-potential children, including the many ways leading donors are already doing so.

Countless lessons and recommendations are sprinkled throughout this volume. Taken together, they outline the current status of education for quick learners, and illuminate some paths forward. In lieu of an executive summary, here are 22 general findings, ideas, and suggestions that emerge from the research for this book.

22 ideas for donors hoping to spur high-achieving students

1. Proselytize for gifted education; it has too few vocal supporters.

2. Underinvesting in top students hinders their ability to fulfill their potential, disadvantages America in future international competitions, and robs everyone of the contributions these individuals can make to society.

3. Though the "average achievement gaps" separating the academic proficiency of various groups of students are slowly closing, the "excellence gap"—the difference in performance at the "advanced level"—is large and growing. Low-income, minority, and English-language-learning students are terribly underrepresented at the highest levels of achievement.

4. Even more worrying, the gap between America's top achievers and top achievers in other nations is yawning wider. This could undermine our whole nation's standard of living and security.

5. Donors could be highly useful in bringing coherence and energy to the education of gifted students.

6. Fuzzy understanding of the population in question is part of the problem, and could be clarified with a bit of research and creation of some recognized standards.

7. There are challenges in identifying students who could benefit from extra stimulation. Some students excel only in one academic sphere, not all. There are highly intelligent students who also have emotional, social, or learning disabilities that mask their potential.

8. A donor need not choose between the needy and the gifted: There are many high-capacity low-income students.

9. Moreover, giving attention to our most academically advanced students may help energize the school reform movement in general—whose biggest beneficiaries by far are the disadvantaged.

10. Before investing, study of existing policies and practices in the target area (school, district, state, or national) is important, because there are no universal standards, and the conditions in one location may have little relation to what is needed elsewhere.

11. Since policies for high achievers will predominantly be set at the state level, investing in and working with state-based organizations is likely to be crucial.

12. Out-of-school enrichment programs currently being run by colleges or non-profits are valuable for identifying and supporting high-potential youth.

13. The charter school sector, which has produced many superior schools, may be ideal for creating institutions capable of stretching talented students (though most state charter laws prevent selective admissions, meaning charters can't gather together a substantial mass of such students on purpose).

14. Public selective-admission "exam schools" can be superb options. However, there are very few of them, and they face numerous operational challenges, including maintaining diverse student bodies and political support.

15. "Acceleration"—advancing a student through her academic career at an above-average pace—can be a highly beneficial and cost-effective tactic. Despite strong research ratification, though, it will sometimes produce polemical opposition.

16. America lags in providing top-level schooling in STEM fields (science, technology, engineering, and math), and this may jeopardize our future economic growth, job creation, and international competitiveness.

17. There are too few high-end offerings in arts education; expanding the number and types of such programs can help engage and advance a segment of the gifted-student population too seldom identified and supported.

18. Online education holds enormous promise for gifted students, because it allows personalization of learning—so fast learners and slow learners alike can find an appropriate lesson pace. Since we are still in the early days of computerized and blended learning, we should be mindful of quality and continue experimenting to find the best models. Some experts worry about placing too high expectations on technological solutions.

19. There is great potential for harnessing colleges to elevate high fliers while they are still in high school or middle school.

Matching at-risk academically talented students with excellent universities could be a high-impact investment.

20. Those most knowledgeable about educating high achievers agree that we need many, many more educators capable of instructing and inspiring our top students. We may need a Teach for America analogue specifically aimed at training teachers to instruct high-potential students.

21. Due to the longstanding neglect of this field, gifted education has a weak research base; entirely too little is known about these students and the interventions that work best. Investments in researchers at policy think tanks and institutions of higher education could shed valuable light.

22. The education needs of top students are all but invisible in federal and state education law and practice. Advocates should try to embed consideration for the needs of high-achievers in public education across the board—in accountability systems, educator evaluations, teacher credentialing rules, charter school laws, and budgets.

SECTION I
On Cultivating Excellence

What is honored in a country is cultivated there.
—*Plato,* Republic, *Book VIII*

Why Students at the High End of the Achievement Continuum Also Deserve Attention

For many good reasons, when the nation focused on K-12 schooling in recent years, conversation and action centered on the plight of low-performing students. Policymakers and philanthropists focused heavily on programs aimed at pulling failing students up to minimum standards. Many of the most successful, prominent, and popular philanthropic investments over the past two decades have financed expansion of opportunities for the lowest-achieving student populations.

That challenge continues to be as pressing as any in contemporary American public life, so nobody wants to push it off the list of donor priorities. However, there are millions of American boys and girls, quite apart from that population that has been the central focus of reform, who are also being let down by today's schools, who are also falling far short of their human potential—simply because most of our schools are not doing an adequate job of stimulating and stretching good students into great students. It is time to allocate greater attention to their cause.

The high-achiever/low-achiever tension is a longstanding, skinned-knee tug-of-war in education circles. But during the last half-century, we seem to have oscillated frenetically between paying attention to the academic needs of high fliers and prioritizing the needs of academic strugglers.

After the Soviet Union's 1957 launch of Sputnik, U.S. policymakers responded with a flurry of math and science programs aimed at pushing the performance of talented U.S. students into a higher orbit.

Then just a few years later, the Lyndon B. Johnson administration built an education policy around the principle that "poverty must not be a bar to learning, and learning must offer an escape from poverty."[1] At the president's urging, Congress created federal programs like Title I of the Elementary and Secondary Education Act that are entirely devoted to lifting up the performance of our most at-risk boys and girls.

After that, Team Equity temporarily lost some ground with rope-burned hands. In 1972, U.S. Commissioner of Education Sidney Marland countered with a report to Congress that too few programs were tailored to the meet the needs of America's most talented students.[2] Then in 1983, the blue-ribbon panel behind the influential publication *A Nation at Risk* gave a mighty tug, warning that schools were not adequately challenging top students: "Over half the population of gifted students do not match their tested ability with comparable achievement in school."[3] Team Excellence—heels dug in, muscles straining—was building momentum.

A decade later, the U.S. Department of Education study *National Excellence: A Case for Developing America's Talent* indicated that most gifted students "continue to spend time in school working well below their capabilities. The

---

1. See Andy Smarick, *The Urban School System of the Future: Applying the Principles and Lessons of Chartering*, Rowman and Littlefield Education, 2012

2. Sidney Marland Jr., *Education of the Gifted and Talented*—Volume 1: Report to the Congress of the United States by the U.S. Commissioner of Education (Washington, DC: Office of Education, 1971), 6. See also Tom Loveless., *High-Achieving Students in the Era of No Child Left Behind*, Washington, DC: Thomas B. Fordham Institute, June 18, 2008, edexcellence.net/publications/high-achieving-students-in.html

3. The National Commission on Excellence in Education, *A Nation at Risk*, 1983

belief espoused in school reform that children from all economic and cultural backgrounds need to reach their full potential has not been extended to America's most talented students. They are under-challenged and therefore underachieve."[4] That depressed everyone in the crowd.

From the early '90s to today, the momentum shifted dramatically, and the tug-of-war became a one-sided affair. Pressed by demands for "equal opportunity," and aghast at the miserable achievement levels of children in our worst public schools, philanthropists and policymakers focused resources on the neediest kids.

Private scholarships, new charter schools, and public programs were almost all tailored to failing students. Court decisions requiring "equity" and "adequacy" funding pushed the attention, and budgets, of administrators in the same direction. The No Child Left Behind Act capped this multifront effort to level the playing field for low-income and minority students, writing into statute demands that schools pull 100 percent of underachievers up to "proficiency," with serious consequences for failure to do so. This left precious little room for progress on other parts of the student spectrum.

Thankfully, significant progress was made in edging low-achievers up toward the average level. For instance, Brookings Institute scholar Tom Loveless found that the "school accountability" era—the period of NCLB and a few years preceding—resulted in substantial performance gains among the lowest-ranked 10 percent of American students. Not enough, for sure, but something to gingerly hang our hats on. Improvement among top-ranked students, however, lagged far behind.[5] Today, Loveless summarizes bluntly, "the United States does not do a good job of educating kids at the top."[6]

> Some people don't think we need to invest much in the most gifted kids; they'll be fine. But that's like saying a great athlete will be great no matter what, so we don't need expert coaches.

4. See Joseph Renzulli, "Is There Still a Need for Gifted Education?" *Learning and Individual Differences*, August 2010. eric.edu.gov/?id=EJ890979

5. Tom Loveless, *High-Achieving Students in the Era of No Child Left Behind*, Washington, DC: Thomas B. Fordham Institute, June 18, 2008, edexcellence.net/publications/high-achieving-students-in.html

6. Amanda Ripley, "Your Child Left Behind," *The Atlantic*, December 2010. theatlantic.com/magazine/archive/2010/12/your-child-left-behind/308310

Now a growing number of experts have begun suggesting that perhaps the pendulum has completed its cycle and ought to begin moving in the other direction. In just the last few years, education scholar Chester Finn co-authored a laudatory book about the nation's selective public high schools, urban education researcher Sol Stern argued in the *Wall Street Journal* that America is shortchanging its best students, and journalist Amanda Ripley published numerous stories on the inability of our best students to compete with their international peers.[7] The slowly mounting consensus seems to be that while our focus on the bottom must continue, it should be matched by increased attention to the top.

Education analyst Michael Petrilli of the Thomas B. Fordham Institute summarizes the argument:

The education reform community has been obsessed with improving the performance of the country's lowest performing students, most of whom were born into poverty and come from disadvantaged minority groups. That's understandable, and even appropriate. But it's not the whole story. America's highest achievers—including those who themselves are poor and/or minority—deserve our attention and concern, too. Partly because a truly equitable system wants all students to learn something new every day. And also because our nation's prosperity and civic health will depend, to a disproportionate degree, on the most academically gifted children now making their way through our schools. They are not well served by our system, and need to be given opportunities to flourish—for their good, and for ours.

Some advocates will recoil from this renewed nudge. "There's a long-standing attitude that, 'Well, smart kids can make it on their own,'" says Brookings scholar Loveless. "After all, they're doing well. So why worry about them?"[8] It is easy "to think that gifted learners don't need

7. See Chester E. Finn and Jessica A. Hockett, *Exam Schools: Inside America's Most Selective Public High Schools*, Princeton University Press, 2012; Amanda Ripley, "Your Child Left Behind," *The Atlantic*, December 2010. theatlantic.com/magazine/archive/2010/12/your-child-left-behind/308310/; Sol Stern. "The Excellence Gap," *Wall Street Journal*, December 24, 2011, online.wsj.com/article/SB10001424052970204464404577116553655745774.html

8. Quoted in Amanda Ripley, "Your Child Left Behind," *The Atlantic*, December 2010. theatlantic.com/magazine/archive/2010/12/your-child-left-behind/308310

additional academic support," agrees the leader of the National Association for Gifted Children.[9]

Bob Davidson, a long-time leading philanthropist in this area, has
found the same sentiment during his years of giving. "Some people don't
think we need to invest much in the most gifted kids; they'll be fine. But
that's like saying a great athlete will be great no matter what, so we don't
need expert coaches."[10]

This "they'll-be-fine" view holds that the future for these children
will be sufficiently bright just due to their natural talents. Dedicating
resources their way, some argue, would come at the expense of other
students and threaten whatever progress we've made in achieving equal-
ity. There is a "good-enough" assumption underneath this view that
neglects both the individual human imperative and the national interest
in seeing a child end up more than just O.K., but rather as good as he or
she can be, and doing wonderful things if possible.

It is disappointing and pernicious that investing in programs
aimed at high-flying kids can occasionally even make a funder the
target of charges of elitism. A recent *New York Times* article on that
city's gifted-and-talented initiative featured critics arguing that such
programs "create castes within schools, one offered an education that
is enriched and accelerated, the other getting a bare-bones version."[11]

It might be argued that American educational policy over the last few
decades has followed the "difference principle" of distributive justice advo-
cated by John Rawls. The late liberal Harvard professor urged that society
should apply its resources only to maximize the standing of those with the
minimum. Efforts to raise the standing of others would only exacerbate
inequalities. In a recent survey, teachers were asked which students were top
priorities at their schools. They were three times likelier to say "academically
struggling" students than "advanced" students. When asked who was most
likely to get one-on-one attention from teachers, 81 percent said struggling
students. Only 5 percent said advanced students.[12]

For sure, the needs of our most vulnerable kids are enormous, and
they deserve as much attention as possible. Donors wanting to focus on
another educational gap, though, (or willing to take a hybrid approach)

---

9. Interview

10. Interview

11. Al Baker, "In One School, Students Are Divided by Gifted Label—and Race," *New York Times*, January 12,
2013, nytimes.com/2013/01/13/education/in-one-school-students-are-divided-by-gifted-label-and-race.html

12. Tom Loveless, *High-Achieving Students in the Era of No Child Left Behind*, Washington, D.C: Thomas
B. Fordham Institute, June 18, 2008, edexcellence.net/publications/high-achieving-students-in.html

will uncover many noble and practical reasons for investing in America's high-capacity students. Moreover, they will find an array of wide open opportunities where giving can make an immediate difference.

Why invest in high-performing students?

The first and most basic reason to invest in programs aimed at our top students is identical to a key motivation for giving to low-performing students: a moral desire to see that every child has a chance to fulfill his or her full potential. When the natural resource of human potential is squandered, that is a loss for the person, her community, and the nation. This is as true for the gifted child who languishes as for any other child.

And it is especially easy for high-potential children to become bored with school or, worse, lose interest in education generally. If she infers that learning will always be easy, she may never acquire hard-to-measure but vital attributes like grit and perseverance. This will bring trouble in her future when she faces challenges in college, graduate school, a job, or family life.

The "drop-off" of high-potential students into mediocrity is far more than speculation. A 2011 study found that, depending on the grade span and subject studied, somewhere between 30 percent and 50 percent of high fliers descend and no longer achieve at the most advanced levels.[13] Research at English schools found that many of their brightest children were also not getting the attention they needed, and as a result 27 percent of previously high-attaining children no longer earned A's or B's in English and math.[14]

Even if a high-potential student ends up with a perfectly fine career and personal life, the delta between what is and what could have been represents a tragic and unnecessary loss of both personal fulfillment and contributions to society. Repeated with lots of potentially high-achieving kids this adds up to dreadful amounts of wasted opportunity. As Chester Finn, co-author of *Exam Schools: Inside America's Most Selective Public High Schools*, has asked, how many of the 5.5 million students who represent the top 10 percent of America's student achievers do you suppose are currently being educated to the max?[15]

---

13. Robert Theaker, Yun Xiang, Michael Dahlin, John Cronin, and Sarah Durant, "Do High Flyers Maintain Their Altitude? Performance Trends of Top Students," 2011, edexcellence.net/publications/high-flyers.html

14. "Schools 'Failing Brightest Pupils'," *BBC*, June 13, 2013, bbc.co.uk/news/education-22873257

15. Chester E. Finn, "Gifted Students Have 'Special Needs,' Too," *The Atlantic*, December 22, 2012, theatlantic.com/national/archive/2012/12/gifted-students-have-special-needs-too/266544

In some families, knowledgeable, insistent, well-resourced parents are able to compensate for undemanding schools. They offer enrichment, find tutors, or supplement the school work of their under-challenged offspring. Some simply decide to home school. But high achievers are born into inattentive families as well as attentive families, poor families along with comfortable families, families where parents know how to compensate and families where they don't. To say high-potential students can just rely on their own domestic resources is unfair, and quite unlike the way we try to help all other children be their best.

Tragically, it is often the talented *low-income* child who finds himself stifled and alienated at a low-achievement school. With neither school nor family fates in his corner, he faces seemingly impassable barriers to intellectual growth and development. He may languish or, worse, apply his intelligence to take himself down some other path much less constructive and more dangerous than what he would have faced in a demanding, aspiring school.

> Our best students lag far behind the high achievers from competing nations. The top 10 percent of American students would be considered middle-of-the-pack in top-scoring countries like South Korea, Finland, and Belgium.

Moreover, when high-potential children get equal attention to their need to be intellectually stimulated, the results can rain gifts on all mankind. "Over the centuries profoundly gifted people have made the largest contributions to society," states philanthropist Bob Davidson, "so it makes sense to invest in them." In an era of stubborn economic uncertainty and acute scientific needs, we could certainly use a few extra Alexander Hamiltons and Albert Einsteins.

For our governments, civic institutions, and domestic economy to thrive, we must constantly replenish our stores of highly talented thinkers and leaders. This is becoming all the more important as the world becomes more complex, faster moving, and interlinked. Whether we like it or not, today we are competing on a world stage when it comes to jobs, investments, intellectual property, scientific discovery, national defense, and other aspects of security and prosperity. Unfortunately, there is reason to believe we are ill-positioned for what's coming.

Unprepared for contests ahead

International assessments of student performance show that American boys and girls now lag behind international peers, especially in the STEM fields (science, technology, engineering, and math) where many of the highest-paying jobs and most important inventions of the future are expected to emerge. Results from the Program for International Student Assessment (PISA) showed the United States in 21st place internationally in science and 30th place in math in 2009.[16] More recent results from two other international assessments found that math and science achievement of U.S. eighth graders was stagnant.[17]

Our best students, worryingly, lag far behind the high achievers from competing nations. As one author recently noted, based on international assessment results, the top 10 percent of American students "would be considered middle-of-the-pack in top-scoring countries like South Korea, Finland, and Belgium."[18] In addition to falling behind the top nations, we are performing below our *own* standards. According to the 2011 National Assessment for Educational Progress (NAEP), only 2 percent of U.S. eighth graders scored at the "advanced" level in science.[19]

Reed Hastings, the founder of Netflix and a major education benefactor (he was once president of the California State Board of Education) told us in an interview that there would be ill consequences if we continue to lag behind other nations. "Human talent is a precious resource. We can't let any of it go to waste, especially as America's international competitors catch up with us and, in some cases, race ahead." He suggested that "a smart investment in programs for the gifted can help more kids reach their full potential, serve our nation's long-term interests, and help close the achievement gap by identifying and supporting high-potential but low-income boys and girls."

---

16. *What Students Know and Can Do: Student Performance in Reading, Mathematics, and Science PISA 2009 Results,* OECD, 2010, oecd.org/pisa/46643496.pdf

17. "Competitors Still Beat U.S. in Math, Science Tests - WSJ.com," online.wsj.com/article/SB1000142412788732433920457817175321519868.html.

18. Laura Vanderkam, *Blended Learning: A Wise Giver's Guide to Supporting Tech-assisted Teaching,* The Philanthropy Roundtable, 2013

19. "NAEP - 2011 Science: Grade 8 National Results," The Nation's Report Card, nationsreportcard.gov/science_2011/g8_nat.asp?tab_id=tab2&subtab_id=Tab_1#chart

Smart investments in our highest-achieving students, as Hastings notes, will also help underprivileged students. In our era of widespread family breakdown and substantial immigration, the Venn diagram of low-income students and high-potential students has substantial overlap. We have opportunities to support at-risk children and stimulate high-potential children at the same time.

Commissioner Marland's report of 40 years ago emphasized this point, noting that because their environments are almost "calculated to stifle potential talent," bright underprivileged kids deserve special attention. In their book *Genius Denied*, Jan and Bob Davidson, the philanthropists who've long invested in high achievers, remind us that while affluent families can always find supplemental programs for their kids, "Poor families are simply stuck with the schools and districts they get."[20]

Indeed, research shows that high-performing high-poverty students can fall through the cracks and regress to the mean at higher rates than their more affluent peers. More optimistic recent findings show that while minority and low-income students are underrepresented among the nation's highest performing students, many of them can remain high fliers over time.[21]

There are all sorts of things a philanthropist might try in an effort to help students at the top while simultaneously closing the achievement gap. Make sure more low-income primary-school students are prepared for rigorous secondary-school work. Increase challenging high-school options like A.P. classes in poor neighborhoods. Help high-achieving students get to and through college. A recent study by Stanford economist Caroline Hoxby and Harvard professor Christopher Avery found that 92 percent of high-achieving, low-income students never even *apply* to the most selective colleges and universities.[22]

The William E. Simon Foundation, whose education program invests primarily in initiatives to increase high-quality educational options and bring about broader systemic improvement through choice and competition, understands the link between gifted education and assistance for the disadvantaged. "Through merit-based scholarships and school choice, philanthropists continue to be crucial in ensuring that talented disadvantaged students have the same opportunities to thrive and

---

20. Jan Davidson, Bob Davidson, and Laura Vanderkam, *Genius Denied: How to Stop Wasting Our Brightest Young Minds*, Simon & Schuster, 2005

21. Robert Theaker, Yun Xiang, Michael Dahlin, John Cronin, and Sarah Durant, "Do High Flyers Maintain Their Altitude? Performance Trends of Top Students," 2011, edexcellence.net/publications/high-flyers.html

22. Caroline M. Hoxby and Christopher Avery, "The Mission 'One-Offs': The Hidden Supply of High-Achieving, Low Income Students," nber.org/papers/w18586

pursue excellence as their peers," says J. Peter Simon, the foundation's co-chairman. "As we all know, many of our nation's great business and public leaders were not born into privilege, but rather their talents were fostered by access to educational programs that challenged them and gave them opportunities to thrive. We need to ensure that the gifted and motivated students of today are afforded the same opportunities."

Broadening the coalition for school reform

A final reason to invest more in our highest-performing students is that this will help politically sustain efforts to improve opportunities for struggling students. First, schools for high-performers can act as cultural magnets for big cities. Middle-income and more affluent families won't feel like they have to leave the city, or shift to private schools, to find an academically demanding setting for their children. This can combat the pernicious effects of segregation and concentrated poverty.

> The school-reform movement may be in jeopardy because it ignored the interests of too many families for too long.

Second, for well more than a decade, most of the resources dedicated to K-12 reform have been funneled into improving outcomes among today's least successful students. There is little thought given to suburban, rural, or middle-class families by today's school reform movement, least of all to children who are fast learners. For years, this was of little moment, but now a predictable backlash has begun.

First there were murmurs that the Education Department's billions of dollars of "Race to the Top" programs offered nothing to non-urban communities. Then, as state budgets tightened, suburban leaders groused more and more about the tax dollars sucked out of their districts. Determined efforts to redistribute great educators from high-achieving schools into low-achieving schools maddened suburban and exurban parents.

The reform community was awakened to this growing storm in the 2012 elections, when pro-reform proposals in a number of states were voted down, and Indiana's state superintendent Tony Bennett, a leader of the national reform movement, was unceremoniously bounced from office by Hoosier voters.

In short, the larger reform movement may be in jeopardy because it ignored the interests of too many non-poor families for too long. All American children and communities need improved education. If 95 percent of the reform energy is poured into 5 percent of existing schools, there will not be broad support for the effort, which is why many promising reforms like choice and charters and alternative teacher paths have failed to become mass movements.

A set of initiatives aimed at producing and supporting high-achieving students will, in addition to being good for countless boys and girls, add a much-needed balance to the current reform agenda. It will signal the reform community's interest in helping *all* students and thereby strengthen a movement that is vital to the disadvantaged but in danger of losing support to the point where it could stall out or even wither.

Marc Porter Magee, founder of the state-based education reform organization 50CAN, spoke to us about these very issues. "Increasingly, we're seeing that if an education reform strategy is to succeed it has to be broad-based and statewide, speaking to the needs of every child," said Magee. "Adding education for high-potential students to the priority list is one important step in building this more comprehensive approach."

In the next chapter, we will assess the current status of education for high fliers. You may find some of this information discouraging at first. Our neglect has had negative consequences, and navigating this field is more difficult than it should be. Savvy donors, however, will see in the weaknesses and challenges I am about to describe an engraved, silver-plated invitation into the field. The current weakness of education for America's top students is a serious problem, begging to be addressed. There is a large and ready upside, though, and enlightened philanthropists are uniquely positioned to lead the charge.

Defining, Defending, and Developing Education Programs for High Achievers

Through life experience, we all learn that one's mental horsepower does not alone determine success in life. There are countless millionaires, prominent writers, and productive inventors who struggled in school. Special abilities come in many shapes, sizes, and permutations, and kids change, develop, advance, and regress constantly.

That said, any sensible person must recognize that some children are not adequately challenged by mainstream schooling, and will never reach their capabilities unless they can be identified and presented with higher demands and supplemental or accelerated instruction. Donors interested in investing in this area might do well to first understand some of the internal debates over who these high-potential students are, and what they need.

Traditional—some might say antiquated—definitions generally identify students using IQ scores. Newer approaches take into account broader measures and aptitudes.[1] The complicated definition now favored by the National Association for Gifted Children falls in the latter category: "Gifted individuals are those who demonstrate outstanding levels of aptitude...or competence...in one or more domains. Domains include any structured area of activity with its own symbol system (e.g., mathematics, music, language) and/or set or sensory-motor skills (e.g., painting, dance, sports)."[2] A cynic might see this as nearly all encompassing. Others might see this as reflecting real life.

Top researchers Franz Monks and Michael Katzko, who are professors in Europe, sketch four broad models in defining giftedness:[3]

- Trait-oriented models
- Cognitive models
- Achievement and performance models
- Environmental models

A trait-oriented approach considers giftedness as a stable, biologically determined personality trait that is identifiable by high scores on intelligence tests. Cognitive models use a "multicomponent" understanding of giftedness that combines intelligence, creativity, and motivation. Achievement-oriented models eschew measures of "natural ability" and focus instead on what an individual actually produces. The antithesis of that is the environmental model, which focuses on factors that inhibit or facilitate the potential for high achievement.[4]

---

1. Ibid.

2. "Redefining Giftedness for a New Century: Shifting the Paradigm," NAGC, nagc.org/index.aspx?id=6404

3. Franz J. Monks and Michael W. Katzko, "Giftedness and Gifted Education," *Conceptions of Giftedness*, eds. Robert J. Sternberg and Janet E. Davidson, books.google.com/books?hl=en&lr=&id=zSZtfDP3t-MC &oi=fnd&pg=PA187&dq#v=onepage&q&f=false

4. Ibid.

Developmental psychologist Howard Gardner's theory of "multiple intelligences" identifies seven "intelligences" that are widely but unevenly distributed.[5]

- Linguistic intelligence includes the ability to analyze information and create products involving oral and written language.
- Logical-mathematical intelligence is the ability to develop equations and solve abstract problems.
- Spatial intelligence is the ability to recognize and manipulate dimensional images.
- Musical intelligence is the ability to produce, remember, and make meaning of different patterns of sound.
- Bodily-kinesthetic intelligence is the ability to use one's own body to create products or solve problems.
- Interpersonal intelligence understands the intentions, motivations, and desires of other people.
- Intrapersonal intelligence entails the capacity to understand oneself, making it easier to keep one's life well regulated.

The thinness in categorical identifiers of potential high achievers might be a call to action for donors willing to support high-quality research and fund new approaches.

Taking care with our identification of gifted students is time-consuming, often confounding, work. But it also represents a genuine effort to deliver on the egalitarian promise of public schooling as it relates to a special group of boys and girls: We will help make the most of the talents of every single child.

Donors particularly sensitive to these issues might decide to invest in tools for identifying students who need extra stimulation. This

Ten states reported spending no state funds at all on gifted education—forget about gifted kids being a priority; they aren't even on the radar screen.

5. Katie Davis, Joanna Christodoulou, Scott Seider, and Howard Gardner, "The Theory of Multiple Intelligences," howardgardner01.files.wordpress.com/2012/06/443-davis-christodoulou-seider-mi-article.pdf

field is still far from an exact science; it needs more attention, more research, and more advocates. Compared to other more heavily investigated fields of education, though, there are greater opportunities for clever and active philanthropists to put a constructive stamp on the state of the art.

State policies: confusion abounds

Alas, once high-potential students have been identified, there are entirely too few programs to serve them. Those that do exist tend to be disconnected from one another and completely unhinged from a central theory of action. No two states have identical strategies. Districts within a state have different approaches. Even individual schools within the same district can have very different programs.

Education for high achievers might be seen as a wayward teen with endless promise: "Wow, it has enormous potential, but it desperately needs a smart, firm guiding hand." That hand could be a donor's. This is particularly true since the public sector has largely withdrawn from this area. What follows is a summarized account of the government's confusion and neglect of top-level students, and what that has begot.

There is no agreement among states today regarding what ought to be provided to high-achieving students, or how those offerings should be funded. In only four states (Iowa, Oklahoma, Georgia, and Mississippi) is gifted programming both mandated and fully funded by the state. Twenty-five states have mandated gifted programming, but districts receive only partial funding from the state. Six states mandate gifted programming but provide no funding whatsoever. Five states make funding available for gifted programming but have no statewide requirements for services. Eleven states and the District of Columbia lack both gifted-education requirements and funding.[6]

Federal laws governing special education (like the Individuals with Disabilities Education Act) establish clear nationwide policies on identifying relevant students, building individualized education plans, providing services, and monitoring compliance. There are no federal statutes, however, to help schools identify and serve especially talented students. The "who" and the "how" of providing education services to high achievers is generally left entirely up to individual districts.

---

6. "Gifted Education Policies," Davidson Institute for Talent Development, davidsongifted.org/db/
StatePolicy.aspx

Nor is there much state-level financing for high-achievers. Of the 36 states that reported their funding levels for gifted-and-talented education in the 2010-2011 school year, fully 10 acknowledged spending no state funds at all. Forget about gifted kids being a priority; they aren't even on the radar screen in these states. The remaining 26 states reported funding levels ranging from $0.03 per student in New Hampshire to $188 per student in Georgia.[7]

The way states staff—or, more often, *don't* staff—gifted education, is a clear indication of its place on the totem pole. Only 17 states reported having at least one state employee devoted full time to gifted-and-talented education. Of those 17, only four have more than one full-time employee, and 27 have some employees allocated part-time to gifted education. Only 15 states have a standing gifted-and-talented advisory committee.[8] Only 16 states publish gifted-and-talented indicators like the numbers of students enrolled in A.P. classes.

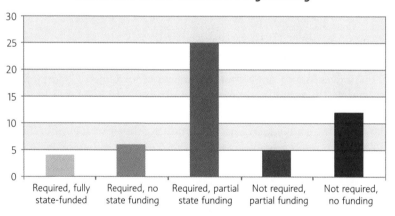

States and Gifted-education Programming

Donors in this area should first spend some time understanding their state's landscape. Executive director Nancy Green of the National Association for Gifted Children suggests beginning at the very top. In states that have a mandate and funding for gifted education, the state department of education typically has a full-time director of gifted programs and services, policies support

---

7. Ibid.
8. Ibid.

acceleration and talent development, principals are more aware of and likely to meet reporting requirements. Districts in these states hire more gifted-education coordinators, more teachers have credentials in educating high achievers, and more quality programs exist. In states that lack a mandate, Green says, it is "as if gifted students don't even exist."[9]

Some specific questions a donor might ask include:

- Does my state have a requirement that schools identify and serve high-achieving students?
- How does my state define them?
- Is there state funding for gifted programs?
- Where does the funding go?
- Are there teachers who particularly focus on stimulating high achievers?

> Only half of states responding to a national survey reported that all of their districts actually identify gifted students.

The Web site of the National Association for Gifted Children has a section entitled "Gifted in the States" that provides information about state-level policies, descriptive statistics, contact information for relevant people at the state educational agency, and links to various associations interested in high achievers. The Web sites of state departments of education sometimes also provide similar information.

Once a donor has a firm understanding of her state's specific gifted-education policies, understanding the state's advocacy environment may be a worthwhile next step. Most states have an advocacy organization dedicated solely or primarily to advancing the cause of high-potential students. NAGC has affiliate associations in 45 states. Other education advocacy groups may also include gifted education among their priorities. These groups can often provide nuanced information about the history, status, and likely future of gifted education in the state. They are also possible vehicles for future advocacy campaigns.

---

9. Interview

An effective campaign in support of high-achieving students almost has to be state-specific. States start in very different places and have very different trajectories, so donors will need to research local conditions before launching any program. The old adage "measure twice, cut once" seems fitting. A donor looking for a big idea in this area may consider a strong advocacy campaign to require the state to define "gifted" students, mandate high-quality local programming for such students, and provide partial or full state funding for these activities.

Sub-groups and high-end education programs

There are subgroups of students for whom classification is especially difficult—for instance, those who are now labeled "twice-exceptional" for being both gifted *and* learning disabled. Children with autism sometimes have special math or computer skills. There are emotional or behavioral disorders that can interfere with or mask intellectual gifts. The "twice exceptional" have "outstanding talents in some areas and debilitating weaknesses in others" that often preclude their identification as gifted, thus denying them the specialized stimulation that could make them fully successful.[10]

Twice-exceptional students require educational services designed to address both areas of need. Interestingly, strength-based programming that focuses on developing a student's talents rather than on remediating his weaknesses has been found to help twice-exceptional students the most. Pulling them from the top rather than pushing them from the bottom of their competency spectrum makes them more capable, increases their desire to succeed, and helps them compensate for their disabilities on a path to achievement.[11]

It's intriguing that when educational efforts for these students are shifted from remediation of their weaknesses to expansion of their unusual talents, their social, emotional, and academic results alike tend to improve. Perhaps there are wider lessons in this. Donors interested in easing skeptical or unknowledgeable school officials into a more receptive attitude toward gifted education might consider funding small programs for this particular subset of students. Supporting research on proper identification and productive interventions for children who are both gifted

---

10. Lilia M. Ruban and Sally M. Reis, "Identification and Assessment of Gifted Students with Learning Disabilities" *Theory into Practice*, Spring 2005, pp. 115-124, jstor.org.proxygw.wrlc.org/stable/pdfplus/3497030.pdf
11. Ibid.

and disabled could be a savvy approach in schools where there might otherwise be resistance to special programming for high performance. Donors could then lever accomplishments among this small population into wider efforts at the high end of the achievement spectrum.

While underachievement will be seen across the entire spectrum of gifted students, there is reason to believe it may be especially pronounced among gifted low-income and minority students. Low expectations, poverty, weaker family supports, and poor urban schools make it especially difficult for high fliers among the disadvantaged to reach their natural altitude in school.[12]

While gaps in average achievement between middle-class and poor children have been slowly closing since the 1970s, there are indications that the "excellence gap" between top performers in each group has been growing.[13] Recent analyses of NAEP scores between 1996 and 2007 revealed this troubling trend:[14]

> While underachievement is a problem across the entire spectrum of gifted students, there is reason to believe it may be especially pronounced among gifted low-income and minority students.

- The gap between white and black students meeting the advanced level in fourth-grade math widened to 6.8 percentage points, with 7.6 percent of white students and only 0.8 percent of black students reaching the advanced level. The gap between white and Hispanic fourth graders at the advanced level widened to 6.1 percentage points, with only 1.5 percent of Hispanic fourth graders reaching the advanced level.
- The gap between white and black students meeting the advanced level in eighth-grade math widened to 8.5 percentage

---

12. Ibid.

13. Jonathan A. Plucker, Nathan Burroughs, and Ruiting Song, "Mind the (Other) Gap! The Growing Excellence Gap in K-12 Education," February, 2010, iub.edu/~ceep/Gap/excellence/ExcellenceGapBrief.pdf

14. Ibid.

Twice-exceptional Students: A First-person Account

All three of my children are twice exceptional. Each is gifted, but between them they also have attention deficit hyperactivity disorder (ADHD), dyslexia, and an auditory processing disorder. We've struggled mightily to find the schools and programs that would serve them well. They've attended traditional public schools, charter schools, magnet schools, a special-education school, even a Canadian boarding school.

We've enriched their curriculum with online courses, dancing lessons, improvisation classes, musical training, athletics, summer academic programs, tutoring, traveling, and more. Our persistence as parents and their hard work as students have paid off. Our oldest starts college at the University of Southern California this fall. Our middle child attends the selective Los Angeles County High School for the Arts. The youngest has found a great spot in a challenging science academy within a large public charter middle school.

It is a rare teacher who is able to identify the twice-exceptional, and current assessments lack the sophistication to identify such students or accurately gauge their progress. Few programs have successful strategies for addressing ADHD, dyslexia, and Asperger's Syndrome—each of which sometimes accompanies giftedness. Much more needs to be done in student outreach, educator professional development, research on program efficacy, and the expansion of successful programs.

—Caprice Young, Ed.D, is former vice-president of education at the Laura and John Arnold Foundation, and former president of the Los Angeles Unified School District

points, with 9.4 percent of white students and only 0.9 percent of black students reaching the advanced level. Only 1.8 percent of Hispanic eighth graders reached the advanced level.

When scores are broken down by economic status (using qualification for subsidized school meals as the low-income indicator) the
data reveal a similar trend:

- In eighth-grade math the gap was 8.3 percentage points,
  with only 1.7 percent of low-income students testing at the
  advanced level, compared to 10.0 percent of other students.
- In eighth-grade reading, 0.6 percent of low-income students
  tested at the advanced level, compared to 3.7 percent of others.

Finally, when the scores of English-language learners (ELL) and
native speakers are compared, the data again show a large and growing gap:

- Between 1998 and 2007 the gap between ELL and non-
  ELL students achieving at the advanced level in fourth grade
  reading widened to 7.8 percentage points, with 0.8 percent
  of ELL students and 8.6 percent of non-ELL students
  scoring at the advanced level.
- In eighth grade reading the gap between ELL and non-ELL
  students achieving at the advanced level widened to 2.7
  percentage points, with 0.2 percent of ELL and 2.9 percent
  of non-ELL students scoring at the advanced level.[15]

Taken together, the data are clear that students from historically underserved groups are far less likely to reach the highest levels of achievement
than their more affluent, white, English-speaking peers. Programs that support, challenge, and elevate top-end learners are thus needed even more
urgently among disadvantaged children than others. Supporting gifted
programs that specifically target low-income or minority students may be
another way for donors to make a non-threatening debut in support for
high-achiever education.

A philanthropist can help schools or system operators reconsider
how they identify students with great academic potential, especially
those who are otherwise likely to be passed over. As education scholar
Chester Finn noted in a 2012 *New York Times* op-ed, "We're weak at
identifying 'gifted and talented' children early, particularly if they're

---

15. Ibid.

poor or members of minority groups or don't have savvy, pushy parents."[16] Most teachers lack formal training in finding and educating gifted students, and thus are often influenced by misconceptions about giftedness. Where there are no clear standards, teachers will often look at good-behavior clues like cooperation, punctuality, and neatness; but these don't always track with high potential. Of the only 29 states that require services to be provided to gifted students, just six have state requirements that regular classroom teachers receive training in educating high achievers.[17]

When you learn that 46 states use teacher nominations in some capacity during their process for identifying high fliers, you can see how thumb-on-the-scale gifted system begins to emerge.[18] The need for dispassionate, reliable, and fair procedures for identifying gifted students is imperative to ensuring that all students have equitable access to programs that match their intellectual needs.

A philanthropist could nudge target districts with simple questions:

- Are you only looking for evidence of previous success, or are you searching for high-potential kids, too?
- Do you have any efforts in place to make sure you're reaching all families?
- Are there barriers to the participation of some students, like challenging applications, entrance fees, or the distance of the program's delivery from a child's neighborhood?

Case study: New York City
Nowhere have conflicts over race, class, and access to gifted programs been more heated—or more public—than in New York City. The fierce competition over scarce seats in gifted programs is perhaps understandable given the district's persistently poor overall performance. NAEP data show New York City struggling mightily; for example, only 24 percent of its eighth graders reached proficiency in reading in 2011.[19] Accordingly, getting your children into one of the district's under-supplied and coveted district-run gifted-and-talented

---

16. Chester E. Finn, "Gifted Students Deserve More Opportunities," *New York Times*, September 18, 2012, nytimes.com/2012/09/19/opinion/gifted-students-deserve-more-opportunities.html

17. "Teaching Gifted Children: National Guidelines and State Requirements," *Duke TIP Digest of Gifted Research*, tip.duke.edu/node/897

18. Ibid.

19. nces.ed.gov/nationsreportcard/pubs/dst2011/2012456.aspx

programs is an enormous priority for many parents who live in the city and send their children to public schools.

Prior to 2008, the gifted identification system allowed each of the city's 32 mini-districts to set its own criteria for admission. In 2008, in an effort to promote "fairness and uniform standards," this system was replaced with a uniform test-based admissions process.[20] This switch gave rise to test-preparation services, from simple booklets that cost just a few dollars to serious preparation classes costing several hundred dollars or more.[21] The number of students eligible for New York City's special programs for high achievers increased by 22 percent from 2011 to 2012, reaching a level of more than double the number from four years earlier.[22]

Despite this expansion, poor and minority children are under-represented in the city's gifted programs. In response, New York City implemented a new entrance test beginning in the 2012-2013 school year, the Naglieri Nonverbal Ability Test (NNAT).[23] It is hoped that student scores will be less influenced by test preparation, spoken language, and similar factors that could depress the participation of disadvantaged kids.[24] The test is designed to focus more on cognitive ability and less on school readiness, which tends to favor students who have had access to a range of supports from an early age.[25]

The new test relies largely on "abstract and spatial thinking and largely eliminates language, even from instructions, an approach that officials said better captures intelligence and is more appropriate for the city's multilingual population."[26] The NNAT will now count for two thirds of a student's score, with the previously used Otis-Lennon School Ability

20. Al Baker, "Slightly Fewer Children Eligible for Gifted Classes in New York," New York Times, April 8, 2013, nytimes.com/2013/04/09/nyregion/slight-dip-in-number-of-children-eligible-for-new-york-citys-gifted-schools.html?_r=1&

21. Anna M. Phillips, "After Number of Gifted Soars, a Fight for Kindergarten Slots," New York Times, April 13, 2013, nytimes.com/2012/04/14/nyregion/as-ranks-of-gifted-soar-in-ny-fight-brews-for-kindergarten-slots.html

22. Ibid.

23. Yoav Gonen, "City's little geniuses: U. Westside has top percentage of 'gifted' kids," New York Post, April 9, 2013, nypost.com/p/news/local/city_little_geniuses_4GJMkQxc6onue5IdzxS65M

24. Al Baker, "Slightly Fewer Children Eligible for Gifted Classes in New York," New York Times, April 8, 2013, nytimes.com/2013/04/09/nyregion/slight-dip-in-number-of-children-eligible-for-new-york-citys-gifted-schools.html?_r=1&

25. Jenny Anderson, "Schools Ask: Gifted, or Just Well-Prepared?" New York Times, February 17, 2013, nytimes.com/2013/02/18/nyregion/new-york-city-schools-struggle-to-separate-the-gifted-from-the-just-well-prepared.html?pagewanted=all

26. Sophia Hollander, "Big Change in Gifted and Talented Testing," Wall Street Journal, October 7, 2012, online.wsj.com/article/SB10000872396390444070104578042783816300100.html

Test (OLSAT), a multiple-choice assessment of abstract thinking and reasoning ability, dropping to only one-third of a student's score.

Perhaps as a result of the change in tests, the number of children qualifying gifted programs seats for the 2013-2014 school year declined by more than 6 percent from a year earlier.[27] The racial and gender breakdowns of qualifying students will not be available until the students actually enroll in the programs in the fall; we will have to see how the latest changes influenced access.

But another serious challenge still lurks about. Nearly 2,000 incoming kindergartners scored between the 97th and 99th percentiles on the assessment, making them eligible for seats in the city's five most selective citywide programs. Yet there are only about 280 available kindergarten seats in these programs.[28] Demand for programs that meet the needs of high-potential students is far outstripping supply. The Parents Alliance for Citywide Education, which was founded in 2011 to advocate for gifted education through coalition building and outreach, is now petitioning the city for more programs in more districts.[29] This could have a twofold benefit: providing more gifted seats overall and making participation easier for qualified students previously kept out because of the long commutes required to reach the programs.[30]

Issues of race are at the forefront of admissions challenges at the city's specialized high schools as well. In September 2012 the NAACP Legal Defense and Educational Fund filed a civil-rights complaint against the city's Specialized High School Admissions test. For the 2012-2013 school year, of the 967 eighth-grade students offered admission to Stuyvesant, a highly competitive New York City high school, just two percent were black and just over three percent were Hispanic.[31] The NAACP is now considering a challenge to the city's gifted admissions process for younger students as well.[32]

---

27. Al Baker, "Slightly Fewer Children Eligible for Gifted Classes in New York," *New York Times*, April 8, 2013, nytimes.com/2013/04/09/nyregion/slight-dip-in-number-of-children-eligible-for-new-york-citys-gifted-schools.html?_r=1&

28. Pamela Wheaton, "Parents petition for more citywide G&T seats." *Insideschools.* April 16, 2013, insideschools.org/blog/item/1000627-parents-push-for-more-gt-seats

29. "Parents Alliance for Citywide Education," change.org/organizations/parents_alliance_for_citywide_education_2

30. Pamela Wheaton, "Parents petition for more citywide G&T seats," *Insideschools*, April 16, 2013, insideschools.org/blog/item/1000627-parents-push-for-more-gt-seats

31. "LDF and Others File Complaint Against New York City Specialized High Schools Challenging Admissions Process," September 27, 2012, naacpldf.org/update/ldf-and-others-file-complaint-against-new-york-city-specialized-high-schools-challenging-admi

32. Sophia Hollander, "Big Change in Gifted and Talented Testing," *Wall Street Journal*, October 7, 2012, online.wsj.com/article/SB10000872396390444070104578042783816300100.html

Though New York City is well known as a cauldron of racial and class contention, donors should be aware that the controversies at play there may pop up in other cities as well. Part of the surveying process we recommended earlier (examining local law, programs, and cultural history) might include a consideration of the receptivity of local citizens in places where you are considering acting. Philanthropists may want to ask tough questions about student recruitment, identification, and access, about enrollment levels, about the location of programs, and about administrative willingness to defend and strengthen programs in the face of potential critics.

After those tests have been met, the next step for the interested donor will be to look under the hood of implementation. Turn your attention to the work itself and ask, exactly what programs can be made available? What will they do? And what is necessary to make them succeed?

▶ Summary of Investment Possibilities

- Work with experts to generate better definitions of "giftedness" and improve the identification of high-potential students within classrooms
- Assess and publicize your state or district policies on meeting the special needs of high fliers
- Advocate at the state level for education of high-achieving students
- Support gifted education advocacy organizations at the state or local level
- Research "twice-exceptional" students
- Improve efforts to identify and support low-income gifted students

SECTION II

Varieties of Philanthropic Investments

Philanthropists interested in investing in the education of gifted students have numerous paths, many of them offering wide-open opportunities to innovate, to have an immediate impact, to accomplish new things, to change lives. For speedy influence, donors can select from a wide assortment of in-school and out-of-school enrichment programs and interventions. If your goal is an even broader and longer-lasting effect, you might consider investing in a specialty school, or in training educators with a particular focus on high-potential students. Donors with an even longer time horizon might educate the public on the crucial importance of helping our top students make the most of their talents, while encouraging public policies which make that possible.

Enrichment Programs

For years, in locations coast-to-coast, local philanthropists and other community leaders have quietly developed and supported programs that identify and boost kids with unusually high potential. Hoping to ensure that gifted boys and girls in their neighborhoods, towns, or states have every opportunity to thrive, these benefactors have often created programs that partner with local school systems yet operate separately. On a parallel track, some colleges have created initiatives to find and cultivate high-capacity youngsters in their home regions. In addition to their benevolent motives, these programs build a supply of future matriculates.

Since both of these types of programs exist to supplement what boys and girls receive in their day-to-day classes, they are colloquially known as "enrichment" programs. The who, what, when, where, and how of such enrichment varies widely. Collectively, the existing programs of this type offer a smorgasbord of tactics from which a donor might pick and choose elements to replicate, so we'll spotlight below a few current examples.

University-based programs open to any exceptional student
Though institutions of higher education have probably always sought out gifted young students, this practice was systematized about 40 years ago. What are now known as "talent searches"—efforts to find pre-college students who can reason at a high level either mathematically or verbally—can be traced back to Julian Stanley of Johns Hopkins University in the early 1970s.[1] Four major programs for academically gifted students grew out of his work:

- The Center for Talent Development (CTD) at Northwestern University serves eight midwestern states
- The Center for Talented Youth (CTY) at Johns Hopkins University serves the northeast and the west coast
- The Talent Identification Program (TIP) at Duke University serves 16 southeast and midwest states
- The Center for Bright Kids (CBK) in Denver serves the mountain states[2]

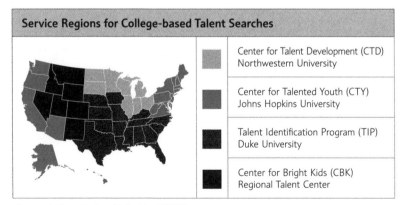

Service Regions for College-based Talent Searches

	Center for Talent Development (CTD) Northwestern University
	Center for Talented Youth (CTY) Johns Hopkins University
	Talent Identification Program (TIP) Duke University
	Center for Bright Kids (CBK) Regional Talent Center

Source: davidsongifted.org/db/Articles_id_10260.aspx

1. "Center for Bright Kids: History," centerforbrightkids.org
2. Interview 4/29/13

These four programs offer a variety of supports for academically talented youth (defined at those who score at or above the 95th percentile on state exams or other nationally normed standardized tests).[3] Once a student is in the program, each center offers additional assessments of student knowledge and capacity using more rigorous exams that far better identify a gifted child's precise aptitude.[4] Elementary-aged students take the EXPLORE test, an above-level, multiple-choice test that measures achievement in English, math, reading, and science. Students in grades six through nine take either the SAT or ACT to test their capacity for post-secondary work. Then independent learning projects, summer programs (day or residential), Saturday programming, or online enrichments are offered to these students to challenge them to reach higher academically.

The ages of students served and the types of supports offered vary by service center. The talent search at Northwestern's CTD is available to students in grades three through nine. However, children as young as four or five are sometimes offered special enrichments.[5] The CTY at Johns Hopkins recruits students in grades two through eight.[6] Duke TIP offers testing and programming for students in grades four through twelve who score in the 95th percentile or higher on a grade-level standardized test, or 125 or above on an IQ test.[7] Depending on their grade levels, students are then eligible for a variety of enriched instructional experiences.[8] At Denver's Center for Bright Kids, students in grades three through nine scoring at or above the 95th percentile are eligible to enroll in summer and academic-year programs. The center offers two programs that continue through a student's junior year in high school.[9]

A fifth institute, the Belin-Blank Center at the University of Iowa, also offers a talent search program, as well as summer programs for gifted students in grades two through eleven. These half-day programs cover a wide range of topics from "Environmental Animation" to "Genetics: How We Are Who We Are." There are programs available for students in grades four through six, middle school students ("Junior Scholar Institute"), and students in grades nine through eleven ("National Scholars Institute").[10] Each

---

3. "Center for Bright Kids: Eligibility," centerforbrightkids.org

4. "Center for Bright Kids: Program Overview," centerforbrightkids.org

5. "Northwestern Center for Talent Development," ctd.northwestern.edu

6. "The 2012-2013 CTY Talent Search," cty.jhu.edu/talent/docs/2012_2013TSbrochure.pdf

7. "Duke TIP: Qualifying," tip.duke.edu

8. "Duke TIP: Students 9th-12th Grade," tip.duke.edu

9. "Center for Bright Kids: Programs," centerforbrightkids.org

10. "National Scholars Institute," www2.education.uiowa.edu/belinblank/Students/summer/programs/9-11/nsi

of these institutes offers advanced-level courses for enrolled students. Additionally, through the National Academy of Arts, Sciences, and Engineering (NAASE), high-achieving students can enroll at the University of Iowa after their junior year in high school.[11] The average NAASE class is small, between 10 and 12 students. This celebrated program attracts students from across the country: approximately 30 percent of students who enroll in the University of Iowa through NAASE come from out of state.

These examples are just a taste. Many other institutions of higher education have programs to identify and educate primary and secondary school students. Philanthropists interested in supporting such university-based programs might contact institutions in their areas of interest (either geographic or according to content) to learn how to bring such opportunities to more children. There are many ways of supporting these programs:

- Increasing their visibility through marketing or publications
- Recruiting, hiring, and retaining expert instructors
- Expanding efforts to identifying eligible students, particularly underserved boys and girls
- Funding scholarships for low-income youth to attend summer programs
- Supporting mentorships or internships
- Starting new programs.

Special programs for high achievers from underprivileged backgrounds

Though institutions of higher education are a logical home for enrichment activities, there are many other ways to launch, house, and operate programs for gifted students. Across the nation, there are many initiatives run and funded by disparate organizations, following different priorities. In this section we will highlight programs that focus particularly on locating and supporting high-achieving students from underprivileged backgrounds. These may suggest strategies that could be supported or emulated elsewhere—for lower-income students, for minorities, or for any child with capacity for high academic achievement.

Next Generation Venture Fund
The Next Generation Venture Fund (NGVF) is a scholarship pro-

---

11. Ibid.

gram that invests in academically talented high school students from African-American, Latino, and Native American backgrounds. It was established in 2003 through a ten-year grant by the Goldman Sachs Foundation, in conjunction with Duke TIP and Johns Hopkins CTY. It later expanded to include Northwestern CTY and the CBK, becoming a national joint venture.[12]

NGVF director Renee Haston says of serving low-income and minority gifted students: "There is a need. Parents are hungry for information. There are a large number of programs for at-risk, underrepresented students, but very few are available for underrepresented students who are gifted. There is a significant need for the latter."[13]

This speaks directly to a point made earlier—that donors passionate about supporting gifted education and helping historically disadvantaged groups of students need not choose between the two or have separate

> There are a large number of programs for at-risk minority students, but very few are available for minority students who are gifted.

strategies; these efforts can be intertwined. The goal of NGVF is to identify and support talented young students from minority backgrounds, help them through high school, and enable them to enroll in and succeed in selective colleges, particularly those deemed "very competitive" or better by Barron's College Guide.

To find candidates, this program partners with the university-based talent searches discussed above. Students who attend summer programs at any of the four talent development centers take the SAT. Seventh graders scoring at the top of the distribution nationally and earning a minimum of a 500 on at least one section are considered for an NGVF scholarship. Students meeting the racial and socioeconomic criteria established by the program are provided an application packet during their eighth grade year. Accepted students then receive nearly $25,000 worth of benefits during their four years in the program.

---

12. "Next Generation Venture Fund," nagc.org/uploadedFiles/Conventions_and_Seminars/Supplemental%20 Programs%20Panel.pdf
13. Interview 4/29/2013

The program includes academically intensive summer camps after the student's eighth- and ninth-grade years. At these camps students pick from a variety of three-week-long accelerated course offerings (with content learning equivalent to a full year of high school or a semester of college). After ninth grade, students attend "Biz Camp," a ten-day entrepreneurial program located at the Duke School of Business. During this session students learn how to create and implement a business plan; they also take college tours and meet with admissions directors and access online and classroom SAT and ACT preparation materials.

One important aspect of the NGVF program is earning the trust and respect of students and their families. Director Renee Haston explains that "to have a successful program, there must be relationship building over time with families. One must have ongoing communication to establish trust and longevity." Program participants are assigned advisers throughout their four years in high school, who hold workshops, communicate with families, and perform on-site school visits to ensure that students are enrolled in and successfully complete a college-prep course load at their high schools. Students are also provided with essay consultants during their senior years to aid in the college application process.

Daniel Murphy Scholarship Fund
The Daniel Murphy Scholarship Fund (DMSF) offers financial assistance and educational support to gifted Chicago students from disadvantaged backgrounds, providing them the opportunity to attend college-prep high schools and benefit from the extracurricular activities and accelerated classes offered there. The fund has five "Core Programs" beginning the summer before students enter high school, and continuing through the college admissions process:

- The Bridge to Excellence Program is a weeklong summer workshop focusing on building students' academic language, organization abilities, time-management skills, and other foundational competencies like note taking and close reading.
- Professional tutors are available to engage with students throughout their high school careers. They provide as-needed support to ensure students' struggles don't stand in the way of long-term success.
- Each student can request a mentor to serve as a role model throughout high school. Additional "affinity groups" provide specialized supports to students.

- The Summer Opportunities program provides summer jobs, internships, cultural and foreign-study programs, sports programs, and community-service work. These build the leadership skills that, when combined with intellectual accomplishment, yield first-rate achievement.
- The College Counseling program includes support for all aspects of the college-application process, including SAT and ACT preparation, application assistance, and guidance through the financial aid process.[14]

DMSF recruits students from across the greater Chicago area through public and parochial schools and community-based organizations. Students apply to the program, and an admissions process that weighs economic need, grades, standardized test scores, writing ability, and teacher recommendations, provides financial aid to about 100 entering ninth graders each fall. These students receive scholarships to attend college-preparatory private and independent high schools in the Chicago area, as well as residential and boarding schools across the country.

One hundred percent of Daniel Murphy scholars go on to college; many attend competitive four-year institutions including Johns Hopkins, Stanford, Yale, Boston College, and Marquette.[15] And many of these students return to the Chicago area and become local advocates for high-performing, low-income students. DMSF recently hired three of its alumni to serve as mentors and affinity-group leaders.

According to DMSF Executive Director Andrew David, one of the best "measuring sticks" for identifying high-quality programs is to track what kids do after they leave. "Are they going to college? Are they persisting through college? What happens when they graduate from college? What happens in their lives? What are they doing in the community? How are they giving back?"[16]

Prep for Prep

Prep for Prep is a non-profit organization that serves high-achieving students of color (African American, Latino, and Asian American) in New York City. The organization's mission is to diversify the pool of young talent so it better reflects the American population. It does this by pro-

---

14. "Daniel Murphy Scholarship Fund," dmsf.org
15. Interview 4/17/13
16. Interview 4/17/13

viding high-achieving students with a superior education coupled with other life-changing opportunities.[17]

There are two parallel tracks that students can take to become Prep scholars: Teachers in public, private, and charter schools in New York City nominate fifth grade students performing in the top ten percent on standardized tests. These students then sit for an assessment administered by Prep for Prep, and an IQ test. The program conducts a family history and multiple interviews before accepting students into the program. Approximately 6,000 students are nominated annually; just 225 are accepted.[18]

Accepted students participate in Prep for Prep's 14-month "boot camp" that occurs the summers before and after a student's sixth-grade year, and on weekends during that year. This boot camp offers both remediation and acceleration for students to help them prepare for placement in New York City's private day schools at the beginning of seventh grade.

The second track begins with teacher nominations of high-achieving seventh graders. These students have the same 14-month boot camp. They are then placed in independent boarding schools in New York and throughout New England.

Summer boot camps serve the dual purposes of preparing students to be academically successful in private and boarding schools and helping students understand the non-academic standards to which they will be held while attending these top-flight schools. Faculty for the summer boot camps are all drawn from independent schools, and each student is paired with an adviser. Advisers are typically Prep for Prep college students who, having gone through the process themselves, are well positioned to prepare students for the academic and social challenges they are likely to face during the transition to independent schools.

Approximately 75 percent of the students who begin a boot camp finish and enroll in independent schools. Once students are placed in day or boarding schools, Prep for Prep continues to provide a high level of support to ensure their success. Each student is matched with a counselor who visits his or her school regularly (once per month for New York City day schools and twice per semester for boarding schools). Students have access to special college counseling services; they participate in a leadership institute; they are offered résumé writing assistance and mock interview opportunities, and helped to compete for internships.

17. Interview 5/21/13
18. prepforprep.org

Nearly 40 percent of Prep's students graduate from Ivy League schools. Nearly all go to competitive colleges. Prep for Prep continues to support its students during college, offering both career-focused opportunities and a large supportive alumni network. The alumni of programs like Prep for Prep and DMSF often go on to prestigious leadership positions and develop a taste for public service. Among Prep alumni are 14 Fulbright Scholarship recipients, two Rhodes Scholars, two Rockefeller Fellows, two Truman Scholars, one White House Fellow, and one Presidential Scholar.[19]

Prep for Prep prides itself on being "unapologetically elite, but not elitist. It's a rigorous leadership-development program for a select and highly targeted group. This small cadre of young people of color is changing people's expectations of who is capable of what all over the country," says Ed Boland, vice president of external affairs. "Our mission is to diversify the leadership pool of this country to better reflect the overall American population, and we have a laser-like focus on that goal."[20] Prep for Prep is a non-profit organization and receives no government grants. Approximately 50 percent of the organization's operating budget comes from its board members; the other half is raised through individual, corporate, and alumni donors and annual events.

The Steppingstone Foundation

In 1990, technology entrepreneur John Simon and teacher Michael Danziger created a new program in Boston that aimed to take "sixth-grade students with high potential but limited opportunities" and prepare them for admission into demanding private schools a year or two later. Then in 1997, their Steppingstone Foundation created another program to prepare the same kind of students for admission into Boston's public high schools that use competitive entrance exams. (We'll discuss public exam schools in detail in the next chapter.) Over the next few years, the foundation created similar programs in Philadelphia and Hartford.

A $400,000 grant given by the L. G. Balfour Foundation in 1994 was important in solidifying and expanding Steppingstone. Their first million-dollar grant, from the Richard and Susan Smith Family Foundation in 2003, led to a fundraising campaign that garnered $19 million in gifts over the next few years. By 2012, Steppingstone had 811 individual donors (147 of whom had given for at least five consecutive years), and 35 supporting foundations, ranging from the Charles Hayden Fund to

19. Ibid.
20. Interview 5/21/2013

Bain Capital Children's Charity. The organization now spends $5 million per year to support 997 students in grades 5-12.[21]

The basic formula is similar to that of Prep for Prep. Children are admitted to the scholars program during the spring of their fourth- or fifth-grade year. Once accepted, they put in hundreds of hours of extra academic-enrichment work outside of school during the summer, the following school year, and next the summer after. Each child takes the Independent School Entrance Exam, and families receive placement assistance and financial-aid counseling. Then every child applies to one of the area's top independent, Catholic, or public exam schools.

Summer boot camps serve dual purposes: preparing students to be academically successful in high school, and helping students understand the academic and non-academic standards to which they will be held in future phases of their lives.

During the 1,000-plus hours that scholars spend in the program over 14 months, Steppingstone both builds on their academic strengths and fills in their academic weaknesses. At present, 90 percent of Steppingstone graduates gain admission to one of the program's 41 selective partner schools—which range from Boston Latin to Xaverian Brothers High School to Phillips Exeter. Nearly all participants graduate from high school, and 80 percent earn a four-year college degree within six years.[22]

Malone Scholars Program

When he was a boy growing up in Connecticut, John C. Malone was awarded a work scholarship that allowed him to attend the Hopkins School, a venerable high-quality private academy in New Haven. According to Malone, this scholarship provided him with "a peer group with whom I could have fascinating and pivotal discussions, an environment where I was not only allowed to be smart but was challenged to see

---

21. tsf.org/wp-content/uploads/2012-Annual-Report.pdf
22. TSF.org

many sides of each issue."[23] Malone traces much of his subsequent success in life to this educational stimulation. He went on to receive a B.A. from Yale and a M.S. and Ph.D. from Johns Hopkins, and eventually became a pioneer in the cable-television business. His self-made personal fortune is estimated at $6 billion, and currently he is the largest individual private landowner in the U.S.

When Malone turned to large-scale philanthropy in the 1990s, his first goal was to provide top students with the same life-changing opportunity for intensive study that the Hopkins School had offered him. The Malone Family Foundation was created in 1997 with the express purpose of improving "access to quality education…for gifted students who lack the financial resources to best develop their talents."[24] Its first large effort was the Malone Scholars Program.

Malone carefully investigated private secondary schools around the country, seeking the most academically rigorous ones. A few at a time, he offered the schools he selected a private endowment, typically around $2 million, that they would use to distribute merit scholarships to exceptionally promising students who lacked the financial capacity to attend the school on their own. Malone eventually endowed scholarships in this way at nearly 50 top-flight private schools.

Through this mechanism, hundreds of "Malone Scholars" have already been able to obtain stiffly challenging high school educations. Many more high-potential, limited-income students will get chances for similar schooling in future years, as the Malone Scholarships continue to be awarded annually.

Jack Kent Cooke Foundation
The Jack Kent Cooke Foundation is a Virginia-based non-profit that was established in 2000 through the estate of self-made billionaire Jack Kent Cooke. He dedicated the bulk of his fortune to supporting individuals of "exceptional promise—those who work hard, stay focused, and defy the stereotype that poverty precludes high achievement."[25] The foundation has a number of programs that support high-achieving, low-income students, including the Young Scholars Program that provides direct scholarships for undergraduate and graduate study, and grants to other non-profit and educational institutions that provide opportunities to these students. The overar-

---

23. riverstoneschool.org/news-events/section-admissions/malone
24. malonefamilyfoundation.com/aboutfoundation_whoweare.html
25. "Jack Kent Cooke Foundation: Our History," jkcf.org/about-jkcf/our-history

ching mission is to ensure that a student's lack of financial resources does not deter him from achieving his very highest potential.

Each year the Young Scholars Program provides 50-75 students (selected from more than 1,000 applicants) with "Individual Learning Plans" tailored to personal talents, educational goals, and financial situation. A full-time foundation educational advisor works with the student and parents or guardians to provide guidance in selecting a high school; support for applying to private or magnet schools; access to summer enrichment programs; acquisition of computers, software, or other learning technologies; specialized support in music, art, science, or other subjects; and resources for career exploration, mentorships, and college advising and counseling.[26]

Students apply to the Young Scholars Program in seventh grade, are accepted in eighth grade, and continue in the program through high school. Applicants are selected predominantly on the basis of their high academic ability and financial need. The review panel also takes into consideration motivation, persistence, and desire to help others through community volunteer work.[27]

The program aspires to develop well-rounded future leaders. That starts with academics. Participants are expected to maintain high grades in honors, Advanced Placement, and International Baccalaureate courses, and to explore music, drama, fine arts, and athletics as well. The program also expects scholars to "act with honesty and personal integrity." They are to maintain clean disciplinary records, show strength of character, and contribute to their communities. Each participant and his parent or guardian are required to sign a letter of agreement that describes these high expectations.

The foundation's college scholarship program provides up to 40 high-performing high school seniors with financial support to attend and graduate from the nation's best four-year colleges and universities. Students with SAT or ACT scores in the top 15 percent nationally can apply. The scholarship includes up to $30,000 in financial support per year for up to four years, and personal advising about the college-selection process, navigating the world of financial aid, and transitioning to college.[28]

The Undergraduate Transfer Scholarship Program makes it possible for the nation's top community-college students to complete their bach-

---

26. "Jack Kent Cooke Foundation: Program Services & Opportunities," jkcf.org/scholarships/young-scholars-program/program-services-opportunities

27. "Jack Kent Cooke Foundation: Selection Criteria," jkcf.org/scholarships/young-scholars-program/selection-criteria

28. "Jack Kent Cooke Foundation: College Scholarship Program," jkcf.org/scholarships/college-scholarship-program

elor's degrees by transferring to four-year colleges or universities. Up to 60 students are awarded scholarships of up to $30,000 per year.[29]

Graduate scholarships make up the foundation's final program that supports students directly. There are two scholarships available through this initiative. The Graduate Arts Award provides 15 college seniors or recent graduates who show exceptional artistic or creative promise up to $50,000 annually for three years so they can complete graduate degrees in the performing arts, visual arts, or creative writing.[30] The Dissertation Fellowship Award helps doctoral students complete dissertations that could aid high-achieving students from low-income backgrounds, or that simply show the potential to be grand achievements.[31] This is a one-time award of $25,000; four to six have been distributed annually in recent years.

A Better Chance enrolls nearly 2,000 academically successful minority, low-income students in over 300 rigorous independent schools or boarding schools in 16 states.

In addition to directly supporting the educational pursuits of high-achieving low-income students, the Jack Kent Cooke Foundation also provides grants to organizations and institutions working to expand schooling opportunities for such students. For example, the Good Neighbor Grants program established in 2012 supports non-profit organizations in the Northern Virginia-DC-Maryland metropolitan area that serve high-achieving kids. Selected grantees receive a one-time award of between $10,000 and $35,000 to be used toward specific program costs.[32]

Another example is the Rural Connections program, a three-year initiative through the Johns Hopkins Center for Talented Youth that is funded by the Jack Kent Cooke Foundation. This program supports

29. "Jack Kent Cooke Foundation: Selection & Eligibility," jkcf.org/scholarships/undergraduate-transfer-scholarships/selection-eligibility

30. "Jack Kent Cooke Foundation: Graduate Arts Award," jkcf.org/scholarships/graduate-scholarships/graduate-arts-award

31. "Jack Kent Cooke Foundation: Dissertation Fellowship Award," jkcf.org/scholarships/graduate-scholarships/jack-kent-cooke-dissertation-fellowship-award

32. "Jack Kent Cooke Foundation: Good Neighbor Grants Program," jkcf.org/grants/good-neighbor-grants-program

bright seventh- through ninth-graders living in rural communities. It provides these students with greater access to CTY's summer programming and other activities.[33]

The Jack Kent Cooke Foundation is a leader in this field. Its executive director, Lawrence Kutner, told us why: "We focus on high-potential, low-income students because they're such an underused resource for making our world a better place. All of us benefit from helping them get the education they need to make the most of their intelligence and talents."

A Better Chance

A Better Chance (ABC) is a New York-based non-profit organization that seeks to increase the number of well-educated people of color who are capable of competing academically in schools, colleges, and the workplace, and of assuming positions of leadership in society. A Better Chance offers its College Preparatory Schools Program to low-income minority middle- and high-school students. The program recruits children of color in grades five through ten. Students apply through ABC, and successful candidates are offered placements in one of over 300 rigorous independent day schools and boarding schools in 16 states and the District of Columbia.

A Better Chance has its roots in the civil rights movement, when in 1963 a group of 23 headmasters of selective independent schools made a commitment to change the composition of their student bodies. In its first year, A Better Chance enrolled 55 minority, low-income, academically successful students in the founding independent schools. Fifty years later, A Better Chance enrolls nearly 2,000 students in over 300 independent schools.[34]

Members of the class of 2012 are 67 percent African Americans, 17 percent Latino, 6 percent Asian American, 1 percent Native American, and 11 percent describe themselves as multiracial or other. About one third of the students come from families living below the poverty line, and many more are from working-class families. Almost half of the participants come from single-parent households.[35]

Approximately 96 percent of A Better Chance graduating seniors immediately enroll in college; 83 percent eventually earn a bachelor's degree, and 50 percent go on to earn a master's or other professional degree. Much like

---

33. "Rural Connections," cty.jhu.edu/scholarships/jack_kent_cooke/rural_connections.html
34. "A Better Chance," abetterchance.org
35. Ibid.

students participating in Prep for Prep or DMSF, A Better Chance alumni often go on to build lofty careers and assume important leadership positions as lawyers, professors, surgeons, elected officials, and executives at multinational corporations like Coca-Cola, Google, and Johnson & Johnson.[36]

In addition to its partnership with over 300 independent day and boarding schools, A Better Chance also has 37 college and university affiliates located in 15 states. These schools work with ABC to facilitate school visits, disseminate information, and support students through the application process.

Individual donors can become involved with A Better Chance through its DreamBuilder program. Relying on annual memberships and larger donations, the program has set a goal of serving 3,500 students annually by 2020.

Local case study: Project EXCITE

The above-mentioned programs and others like them generally have a large geographic scope. However, there are ways to achieve the same goals while working on a smaller scale. A good example is Project EXCITE.

Begun in 1998, Project EXCITE is a collaborative project between the Center for Talent Development at Northwestern University and Evanston/Skokie School District 65 in Illinois. The program was created to address the glaring underrepresentation of minority students in honors and A.P. courses at Evanston Township High School—and the lasting consequences of that underrepresentation.

To this end, Project EXCITE begins working with students in third grade, based on the premise that "the underrepresentation of black and Latino students in honors and A.P. math and science courses is preventable through early intervention."[37] The program provides supplemental educational opportunities in math and science over six years to ensure that by the time students complete eighth grade they will have completed Algebra I (the gateway to higher-level math courses like statistics and calculus), have had exposure to significant laboratory and science experiences, and are prepared for honors-level high school courses in math and science.

Project EXCITE currently serves approximately 130 students in grades three through eight from five participating elementary schools in the Evanston School District. At the beginning of the school year, minority students receive an invitation to participate in the selection process. In October of the

---

36. Ibid.
37. "Project EXCITE," ctd.northwestern.edu/excite/program

same year, applicants take reading and math tests from the Iowa Test of Basic Skills (a nationally normed assessment) and the Naglieri Nonverbal Ability Test (discussed earlier in the New York City case study).

From the initial pool, 20-25 students are chosen based on test performance, classroom achievements, and teacher recommendations. Students enroll in Project EXCITE and begin receiving enrichment services in late November of their third-grade year. These include after-school, weekend, and summer enrichment classes; tutoring; practice and prep for high-school math placement exams; and educational guidance and counseling.

The program's after-school classes are held one afternoon per week at the local high school. Math and science teachers immerse participants in hands-on activities involving biology, chemistry, mathematics, and physics. Saturday Enrichment Programs are held on the Northwestern University campus for students in grades four through eight. Not only do the students get access to top-flight activities, they are also introduced to a college campus early in their academic careers—a strategy used by some of the most successful high-performing high-poverty schools.

Students participate in eight Saturday morning and/or afternoon courses. Those in grades four and six take an integrated math and science class created specifically for Project EXCITE students. Students in grades five, seven, and eight take one of the mathematics or science enrichment courses offered at Northwestern University to any high-performing student from the Chicago area.

During the summer, EXCITE's third and fourth graders participate in reading and math programs that aim to improve basic skills. Fifth graders participate in a summer reading program offered by the Evanston Public Library. Students in grade six participate in Apogee, a three-week math or science program at Northwestern. Seventh-grade students participate in a three-week science program at Evanston Township High School, designed to give them significant laboratory-science experience. Students spend one week each on biology, chemistry, and physics. Finally, eighth-grade students participate in the Summer Bridge Program at the high school. This course is designed to give students a jump-start on the coursework they will take as freshmen and get them accustomed to the high-school environment and expectations. Topics taught include advanced math (Algebra 2/Geometry), and students apply what they learn to physics-related projects.[38]

---

38. "Project EXCITE: Program Components," ctd.northwestern.edu/excite/program/program-components

Project EXCITE is free for participants. The cost of the program is underwritten primarily by Northwestern University, with additional funds from the Evanston/Skokie School District and donations from corporations like AT&T, Citicorp, Coca-Cola, and Morgan Stanley.[39]

Best of all, the results have been tremendous. According to Rhoda Rosen of the Center for Talent Development, in third grade, African-American and Latino students in this district lag behind their white peers in math by 39 and 37 points respectively, on average. By seventh grade those gaps grow to 46 and 38 points for non-EXCITE students. But for those who've participated in EXCITE, the gap is only 4 points. The benefits continue: By ninth grade only 27 percent of non-participating minority students in the high school are working above grade level, compared to 77 percent of EXCITE participants.

This type of locally focused partnership could be a model for donors across the nation. Identify useful supports for gifted kids, set a clear goal, tailor a program for a school or small district, and then engage local schools, colleges, external support organizations, and a range of donors. What's working in Evanston could easily be replicated in Erie, Eureka, or El Paso.

Common features

In the table on pages 62-63, we summarize the primary offerings of the six community-based programs described above. The programs we have highlighted are in no way an exhaustive group or representative of all the possibilities. The ones we've profiled in this section all concentrate on increasing high achievement among minorities. But most of their approaches would work just as well if offered to any child with indications of high academic potential. So prospective donors may find it useful to study some of their similarities.

Each of these programs has a disciplined focus on a tight scope of services. Each assiduously avoids steering outside of those lanes or blurring its mission. This enables each program to develop, refine, and perfect its set of services in order to best support its students. The Jack Kent Cooke Foundation is the exception in providing a wider array of offerings. Its mission is to support gifted poor and minority students all along the educational continuum. For larger donors or for those who intend to dedicate a significant portion of their philanthropy to gifted education,

---

39. "Project EXCITE: FAQs," ctd.northwestern.edu/excite/faq/#faq282

this expanded-front approach might offer the opportunity to substantially extend influence.

The critical first step for funders interested in supporting enrichment programs for gifted youth is to develop clarity in five areas:

- What is my desired geographic focus?
- On which set of gifted students am I going to focus?
- What services do I want to provide?
- What outcomes am I trying to achieve?
- How will I measure performance?

▶ Summary of Investment Possibilities

- Support or expand university-based "talent search" organizations, including expanding recruitment efforts among hard-to-reach families
- Create new or support existing programs designed to identify gifted students and ensure their college matriculation and graduation
- Create new or support existing organizations that focus on identifying and advancing high-potential students in high-priority subjects such as STEM
- Provide scholarships to low-income gifted students so they can attend high-performing, selective high schools and top-tier universities
- Establish a partnership with a district or charter-school network to better identify gifted students and provide advanced classes, tutoring, and other supports
- Given the existing prioritization of middle- and high-school students, develop new programs aimed at identifying and cultivating high-potential elementary students
- Support research to identify the highest-impact enrichment programs and interventions
- Expand the reach of successful programs so they can serve more gifted students in more ways

Comparision of services offered by some enrichment programs for high-potential students

	Supplies academic support in early grades	Supplies academic support in high school	Offers scholarships to independent high schools	Provides support during college application process
Next Generation Venture Fund		✓		✓
Daniel Murphy Scholarship Fund		✓	✓	✓
Prep for Prep		✓	✓	✓
Steppingstone Foundation	✓	✓	✓	✓
Malone Scholars Program		✓	✓	
Jack Kent Cooke Foundation		✓		✓
A Better Chance		✓	✓	✓
Project EXCITE	✓			

Offers college scholarships	Gives grants to other non-profits	Operates within schools rather than outside of school	Funded foremost by philanthropy rather than government money
		√	√
		√	√
		√	√
			√
		√	√
√	√		√
		√	√
		√	√

Whole-school Models

One enduring debate related to gifted education concerns which students we should focus on. There is a line of thought that we should particularly watch out for the preternaturally gifted, and make sure they don't get lost in the shuffle. Few teachers will come upon a budding Isaac Newton, with the natural wherewithal to invent calculus and unwind the mysteries of the universe from his rural English cottage. But statisticians tell us a child with a genius IQ of 145 occurs in the population roughly once in a thousand; a super-genius score of 160 occurs once in ten thousand. So among America's 50 million students, we have tens of thousands of geniuses, and thousands of super-geniuses.

Very few schools put any thought into particular ways of accommodating these unusual children. Profoundly gifted students are thus often isolated in their own little world while in school, where many of the normal offerings have scant relevance or meaning for them. That's why philanthropists like Jan and Bob Davidson primarily support efforts to identify and cultivate such otherwise unsupported rarities.

A different approach says that in most schools there are substantial numbers of students who, though not geniuses, could reach high levels of achievement if reached with the right supportive interventions and high demands. The model here, rather than Newton, might be Thomas Edison—who famously opined to *Harper's Monthly* that genius is 1 percent inspiration and 99 percent perspiration.

Embracing one or the other of these worldviews is likely to lead a philanthropist to different educational approaches.

The perspiration-over-inspiration philosophy suggests that we ought to attempt to reach and support far more children with high-expectation curricula and instruction. By searching harder for different types of special talents kids possess, and then unapologetically applying practical supports premised on pulling them up toward their peak potential, we should be able to grow the nation's supply of highly talented students.

If a donor chooses this path, she might help create schools (or modify existing ones) that use a whole-school enrichment strategy—students are carefully assessed for their interests and gifts, and then offered access to specialized curricula designed to make the most of each child's abilities. The so-called "Schoolwide Enrichment Model" (SEM) is one method for raising expectations and offerings for substantial numbers of students. Extraordinarily rigorous open enrollment charter schools like BASIS and Great Hearts Academies, in which all students are exposed to an advanced course of study, are superb examples of a closely related approach. In addition to the best charter schools, many, many private schools follow this path, which we'll describe below.

A different approach might be appropriate for philanthropists partial to supporting the smaller cohort of profoundly gifted students (some of whom have single-handed potential to dramatically enhance the lives of their fellow citizens through extraordinary insights or creations). The capacity and curiosity of these students require an uncommon level of attention. One pioneer in gifted education has argued that a child with a 140 IQ wastes half of his time in a normal elementary school, while a child with a 170 IQ wastes virtually all of his time there.[1] This has led to the development of a few specialized schools for the highest-potential students.

There are many ways for philanthropists to proceed down either of these two paths. To examine some of the issues that will be encountered in each approach, we will examine one prominent enrichment model and a few specialty schools in the pages that follow.

Bell Academy as an example of school-wide enrichment

Educational psychologist Joseph Renzulli is one of the nation's foremost researchers in the field of gifted education. He has been grappling with many of the issues presented in this book—how to define giftedness, what programs and models best serve high-potential students, and so forth—for more than 30 years. In 1976 he published a seminal article on a whole-school enrichment approach. In it, he argued that there are two types of giftedness: "schoolhouse giftedness" (succeeding in the classroom) and "creative-productive giftedness" (a less understood but important kind of mental inventiveness).[2] These types are not mutually exclusive; in fact, they often overlap. Both are valuable to society, and both require support if the child in question is to develop fully.

To aid such children, professor Renzulli created the "Schoolwide Enrichment Model" (SEM). He explains that accelerated academic programs alone "produce good lesson-learners but not necessarily productive individuals. We want to instill interest and passion and a mindset for creative and investigative modes of learning in our kids, alongside a challenging academic course load."[3]

His school-organizing plan is designed to improve academic achievement, student engagement, and the skills and enthusiasm of teachers. Your author had the opportunity to see Renzulli's Schoolwide Enrichment Model in operation at Bell Academy, in Queens, New York, a traditional public school serving a diverse population. According to New York's reporting system, Bell Academy's performance has been strong, and members of the school's leadership team are excited advocates for the approach.

It appears that a large part of SEM's attraction for educators is its explicit openness to all students. In the words of Renzulli and his collaborators, it "is

---

1. Jan Davidson, Bob Davidson, and Laura Vanderkam, *Genius Denied: How to Stop Wasting Our Brightest Young Minds.* Simon & Schuster, 2005

2. Joseph S. Renzulli and Sally M. Reis, "The Schoolwide Enrichment Model: Executive Summary." gifted. uconn.edu/sem/semexec.html

3. Interview

built around a commitment to…applying the pedagogy of gifted education to enrichment learning opportunities for all students."[4] SEM provides specific enrichment and differentiated teaching strategies alongside the traditional practices of a school. The model is simply a way to extend enrichment opportunities to a larger portion of the general student body.

Bell Academy offers three levels of enriched learning. First, all students are exposed to general exploratory activities called Type I enrichments. These are designed to introduce students to a wide variety of disciplines, topics, occupations, hobbies, persons, places, and events that would not ordinarily be covered in a regular curriculum. Examples of common Type I enrichment activities would be having guest speakers, taking mini-courses on side topics, viewing demonstrations or performances, using rigorous Web-based resources, and going on actual or virtual field trips. These are considered successful if a larger portion of students become attached to a specific field of study and therefore become more engaged in their own educations.

Type II enrichment activities are primarily designed to promote deeper thinking. These are provided to small groups of students within a classroom, often based on interests piqued during Type I activities. This is when students begin to indicate their natural strengths and proclivities and when teachers begin to truly customize instruction. More advanced research or training in a specific content area would be a typical Type II project. Scientifically interested students, for instance, might dive into physics or human anatomy. Students showing a gift for writing might be exposed to more sophisticated texts.

But Type II activities also teach students a range of "process skills" like pattern-finding, summarizing, and determining bias. They train students in self-reliance, understanding nonverbal communication, and dealing with stress. They help students learn how to make inferences, categorize notes, and analyze data. All in all, the goal of this phase is to enable stu-

High achievement comes from an "interaction among three basic clusters of human traits: above-average ability, high levels of commitment, and high levels of creativity."

4. See Renzulli and Reis, "What is the SEM and How Can Implementation be Explored?"

dents to acquire the knowledge and hone the skills they will eventually need to independently pursue their academic interests at a high level.[5]

Type III enrichment engages students who have become invested enough in a self-selected area of study to be willing to commit time for advanced training. Areas for inquiry are chosen by the students with educator support. Students interested in the hard sciences might gather and analyze their own experimental statistics. Students who have enjoyed creative writing might author articles for publication. As with Type II activities, the acquisition of particular skills—not just content—is essential. So, for example, students learn how to direct their own learning by improving planning, organization, resource use, and time management. A key element of Type III enrichments is that they are pursued with the goal of having students share the products of their study with an audience larger than the classroom. The objective is to demonstrate to students who are ripe to the understanding that learning has a higher purpose than just schoolhouse grades.

It is important to note that students continue to receive a standard course of study. A participating school would still teach to the state's content standards in various subjects, and administer the state's assessments. But under the schoolwide enrichment approach, the regular curriculum is supplemented and adjusted; for example, the difficulty level of required materials would be differentiated for student groups, and extra enrichment activities would folded in. In short, the "goal in the SEM is to influence rather than replace the regular curriculum."[6]

Bell Academy aims to expose all of its students to Type I enriched-learning opportunities. Then a "talent pool" is identified—above-average ability, high-potential students whose imaginations have been captured. In an effort to ensure that students with a variety of talents and potential are included in the talent pool, multiple identification measures are used. These include teacher nominations, parent nominations, student essays, a gifted-learning inventory, students' report cards, state exam scores, and the Otis-Lenin School Ability Test (OLSAT), which measures verbal, quantitative, and spatial reasoning.

These multiple measures increase the chances of homing in on each student's strengths, and reduce the chances that a child with the potential for extraordinary excellence might fail to be identified. Bell Academy students with soaring test scores are automatically included in the talent

5. Taxonomy of Type II Process Skills, gifted.uconn.edu/sem/typeiips.html

6. The Schoolwide Enrichment Model Executive Summary, gifted.uconn.edu/sem/semexec.html

pool. But there are also plenty of other opportunities to find areas of high potential in students.

High achievement, Renzulli suggests, comes from an "interaction among three basic clusters of human traits: above-average ability, high levels of commitment, and high levels of creativity."[7] The Bell Academy approach seems effective at cultivating creative-productive giftedness in students, rather than simply stopping at academic talents. In America's entrepreneurial economy and society this may be especially important. For, as Renzulli says, "American productivity comes from people with ideas."

Bell Academy's academic record is very strong. On the city's most recent school report card, it received an A for student performance and outperformed 74 percent of New York City middle schools.[8] It accomplishes this with an extremely diverse student body: nearly half of its students qualify for the federal free and reduced-price lunch program, and its population is split about evenly among Hispanic, Asian, and white students.[9] Bell's results aren't unique. According to the Neag Center for Gifted Education and Talent Development, research on the Schoolwide Enrichment Model suggests that it "is effective at serving high-ability students in a variety of educational settings and in schools serving diverse ethnic and socioeconomic populations."

What may be most encouraging is that this model is easily replicated. There are several steps for any school wanting to implement SEM: Initial program planning and staff instruction will be offered right at each school, over about two weeks and at a total cost of $30,000-$40,000. The school's teachers get trained at Renzulli's summer institute at the University of Connecticut, usually spread over two or three years (at a total cost of $1,350 per teacher or principal). Some special math and reading course materials must be purchased (less than $15 per student and $30 per teacher). For $5,000, a school can purchase a school license for an online enrichment program that all students, teachers, and parents can access.

The Schoolwide Enrichment Model has been implemented in more than 2,500 American schools, and even more overseas.[10] Its reach is being extended by new technological tools provided by Renzulli Learning. A stu-

---

7. Ibid.

8. New York City Department of Education Progress Report 2011-12, schools.nyc.gov/OA/ SchoolReports/2011-12/Progress_Report_2012_EMS_Q294.pdf

9. The New York State School Report Card, Accountability and Overview Report 2010-11, reportcards. nysed.gov/files/2010-11/AOR-2011-342500010294.pdf

10. Neag Center for Gifted Education and Talent Development, Schoolwide Enrichment Model, gifted. uconn.edu/sem

dent completes an online questionnaire, and then software builds a profile of his interests and learning styles. This can then be used to determine which of 40,000 online resources are best suited to advance his learning.[11]

The successes of rigorous charter schools
BASIS Schools

The increasingly lauded BASIS charter school network has 10 campuses located throughout Arizona. In 2012 the network opened its first school outside of Arizona, in Washington, D.C., and it expanded again in 2013 to San Antonio in Texas, for a total of 12 schools. We visited the BASIS school in D.C. during the spring of 2013, and spent some time talking with network co-founder Michael Block. The facility is located in a former office building in D.C.'s busy downtown area.

> "There's no magic here. It's just a four-letter word: Work. We just work harder."

All BASIS charter schools have three core components: Tuition-free open enrollment, a world-competitive curriculum, and internationally recognized testing. Beginning in fifth grade, students are exposed to a challenging, accelerated curriculum focused on content mastery. Craig Barrett, former CEO and board chairman of the Intel Corp., has been a key philanthropic supporter of BASIS. He explains in an interview that "We start on the premise that any fourth-grade child who is at grade level can come to BASIS and succeed in our accelerated program."[12]

How do they do it? Says co-founder Michael Block, "There's no magic here. It's just a four-letter word: Work. We just work harder here."

BASIS schools administer a rigorous, A.P.-based curriculum across the board to all students. All content areas are highly challenging.

The network's intent is to challenge every single student. This approach truly embodies the view that our supply of high-achieving students is not fixed by nature but can be built up. "We have been severely underestimating *all* kids," argues Block.

Science is a particular focus of BASIS schools. In sixth grade, students begin taking biology, chemistry, and physics as separate subjects.

---

11. Renzulli Learning, "What is Renzulli Learning?," renzullilearning.com/whatisrenzullilearning.aspx
12. Interview 4/31/2013

This mirrors the demanding course schedule of many top-performing European and Asian schools. On my tour, I observed an exhilarating sixth-grade biology course led by an outstanding teacher. She moved at lightning speed while keeping a tight hold on all 22 sets of young eyes. They responded swiftly to her questions about parts and functions of the brain—"parietal lobe," "temporal lobe," "Broca's area!"

Math is also a heavy focus in BASIS schools. All students will have completed Algebra I by the end of their seventh-grade year. Amazingly, some seventh-graders will have completed Algebra II or Pre-Calculus. Indeed, I saw an Algebra II class that included eighth-grade students, seventh-grade students, and even one sixth-grade student.

Beginning in sixth grade, students are required to pass comprehensive exams in all core subjects in order to be promoted to the next grade. All students take Latin in fifth and sixth grade. In seventh grade, students may choose to continue Latin or take a modern language like French, Mandarin, or Spanish.

Eighth grade is used to prepare students to enter a rigorous high school program. Students take World History II; the A.P. World History exam is used as the comprehensive exam for this course. It is the first of many A.P. exams BASIS students take. In math and English, the International General Certificate of Secondary Education is used as the end-of-year exam. These exams are subject specific, recognized internationally, and known for their reliability as true records of attainment. Exam scores count for half of a student's final course grade.

The BASIS Upper School (grades 9-11) offers a highly accelerated science and liberal arts program. The core curriculum requires students to take A.P. courses (the equivalent of serious college-level work) and A.P. exams. Because of the school's high expectations, BASIS students have met the entry requirements for most four-year colleges by the end of eleventh grade. A student thus has several options for her senior year: She may graduate early and move on to college. Or she may enroll in a twelfth-grade that is divided into trimesters: the first two offer "Capstone Courses," and the third semester is dedicated to completing a senior project.

Capstone Courses dive deeply into advanced material equivalent to mid-level college courses: topics such as organic chemistry, quantum mechanics, differential equations, and game theory. The senior project encourages students to apply what they have learned in high school to an individualized, mentor-assisted, independent project. These are often carried out beyond campus; senior projects have included everything from internships in university research labs to field work abroad. Theses ranging from "Immigration Laws in the U.S." to "Molecular Gastronomy" have been submitted as senior projects.

BASIS relies on the extraordinary content knowledge of its teachers to ignite in students a passion and curiosity for learning—and to have the chops necessary to teach such accelerated courses and respond to the high-level questions of students. The network's leadership believes firmly that due to BASIS's rigorous coursework, placing content experts in the classroom is essential. "That's our secret sauce," explains Block.

You are likelier to find a retired electrical engineer or a specialist in literature than a conventional teacher-school graduate leading classes in a BASIS school. (In Chapter 7, we provide a full treatment of the role of educators in gifted education.) To build the right culture and expectations from the start at the new BASIS satellite in D.C., the network imported several experienced instructors from its Arizona flagship schools.

BASIS negotiates an initial salary individually with each teacher. It also offers performance-based financial incentives. Teachers of A.P. courses, for instance, earn an additional $100 for every student who earns a grade of four on the A.P. exam, and an additional $200 for every student who earns a five.

Rather than traditional sick days, BASIS gives teachers a "Wellness Bonus" of $1,500. They lose a pre-determined amount of that for each sick-day taken. As a result, the network's teachers miss fewer days than in other teaching institutions.

Teachers are not released for professional development during the academic day. "We are very serious about what we do. The academic day is the academic day. The academic year is the academic year," explained founder Block during our tour. When students are present, instructors are expected to focus on them intently.

The results of all of this are outstanding. On the 2012 Arizona Instrument to Measure Standards (AIMS), the state's end-of-year assessment, BASIS students outperformed statewide averages in math, reading, writing, and science in every tested grade. In 2012, BASIS students outscored national averages on A.P. exams in 23 subjects. Approximately 1.5 million American students take the PSAT test every year, and on the basis of its scores about one percent of all high-school seniors are selected as National Merit Scholar Finalists. In 2012, more than 25 percent of all BASIS seniors earned that high recognition. The performance of BASIS schools on the inaugural international assessment using PISA tests that I discuss in the final chapter of this book shows that BASIS students are competitive with the very best scholars anywhere in the world.

The PISA results are fitting. For the mission of BASIS is to ensure that their students are not just college-ready but also ready to go toe-to-toe with the brightest students across the globe. "We wanted to prove that American schools could offer students a world-class education," explains Block.

Fully 60 percent of all of the 2012 graduates from BASIS schools earn three or more A.P. scores of 5 (a perfect score).[13] That is equivalent to the high school performance level of students who succeed at the world's most selective colleges. For tuition-free, open enrollment schools that do not cherry-pick students, that is an amazing fact.

Though they have to date focused on middle schools and high schools, BASIS is now piloting a kindergarten-to-fourth-grade school in Tucson. So a full K-12 system may soon exist under the BASIS model. The network's major goal is to maintain its extremely high and consistent level of quality as it continues to grow. And growth is a high priority for the network's leadership. "All cities should have a BASIS," I was told at the end of my visit.

It was philanthropic support that built BASIS to its current status, and philanthropic support will be crucial in continuing to expand the system. Moreover, it will largely be philanthropic money and energy that determines if there are to be other schools that emulate BASIS, and bring its now-proven philosophy to more students in new places.

All new charter schools involve startup costs—expenses that must be paid before per-pupil state funds arrive alongside students in the fall. New cities must be scouted and selected, facilities must be identified, acquired, and often rehabilitated. Teachers must be recruited, hired, and trained. Supplies must be purchased. Back-office systems—payroll, benefits, student databases, procurement—must get off the ground. Philanthropic dollars are essential to cover these costs.

Because of serious barriers in some states' charter school laws (like requiring standard teacher certification even if a potential teacher is a recognized content expert), BASIS is considering starting certain new campuses as private schools. In 2009, the organization created a for-profit management organization that helps to operate the network's schools; it will be the vehicle for launching any private-sector

---

13. BASIS 2012/2013 brochure

school. If BASIS pursues this option, private funding will be even more important. All of the startup costs associated with operating in the charter sector will be present, and, unless they participate in one of the too few state-level voucher or tuition-tax-credit programs, they will receive no stream of public funds. Donated funds will be crucial to keeping tuition affordable.

Philanthropists might think about extending BASIS's remarkable results in two other ways. First, there are charter school "incubators" like New Schools for New Orleans and Minnesota's Charter School Partners that help plant local schools by identifying a future school leader, training her and her staff, finding a building, and helping with other activities necessary for opening a charter school. To date, these incubators have focused on pulling up the lowest levels of school achievement. Private funds could encourage and help these incubators start super rigorous BASIS-like schools as well. David Harris, founder of the Mind Trust, a charter incubator in Indianapolis, told us his group would consider such efforts. "It's critical to help our best students—particularly high-achieving students from challenging circumstances."

Second, philanthropic dollars could support the dissemination of BASIS's lessons to other schools: charter, traditional public, and private. The means might include sponsoring fellowships for teachers and principals to work at BASIS for a year, or publishing case studies on aspects of the BASIS model, or creating videos that capture its successful classroom practices.

BASIS certainly wouldn't be where it is today absent the generosity of private benefactors. Former Intel Corp. CEO Craig Barrett, who has been intimately involved in an array of education reforms (such serving on the boards of the groups K12 and Achieve), was an early donor to BASIS along with his wife ambassador Barbara Barrett. After being wowed by the Scottsdale campus in 2006, the Barretts became founding contributors to the school's Master Teacher Campaign which helped it expand and recruit and retain its exceptional faculty.

BASIS continues to rely on donor support of its annual teacher fund, which allows the network to pull gifted professionals into teaching, and offer them adequate compensation to keep them in the classroom as they progress through their careers. The network's expansion to Texas was also philanthropically underwritten. With funding from the George W. Brackenridge Foundation, the Ewing Halsell Foundation, local philanthropist Will Harte, and other givers, the San Antonio non-profit Choose to Succeed convinced BASIS and other standout charter school operators like KIPP, Carpe Diem, and Rocketship to bring their formulas to south Texas.

Great Hearts Academies

The Phoenix metropolitan area has also produced another free, public, charter school network that exhibits astounding success at pulling very high levels of achievement out of many of its students. The first Great Hearts Academy opened in 2002. It was designed to offer a high-demand, academically rigorous, classical liberal arts education with an emphasis on the great books. By 2013 there were 16 Great Hearts Academies in the Phoenix area, and two more schools set to open for the 2013-2014 school year, including one in Texas. There are currently more than 9,000 students on waiting lists hoping to attend a Great Hearts school.[14]

Great Hearts has built "a new model for public education that can be used across the spectrum to bring great results and cultivate great American students from wherever they begin," says donor and co-founder Jay Heiler. "There are high-capacity kids in every corner of our society; they

> There are high-capacity kids in every corner of our society; they exist everywhere. We need to create structures to allow human talent to express itself and grow.

exist everywhere. Human talent is not scarce. It is endlessly abundant and we need to create structures to allow human talent to express itself and grow."[15] Like BASIS, Great Hearts doesn't view high-achieving students as some unalterably fixed quota, but as a group that can be inculcated and expanded.

Heiler echoes the argument made in this book's introduction that paying attention to potentially high-achieving students is a necessary condition for continuing to help the most disadvantaged students and closing the achievement gap at the other end of the achievement spectrum. "For years, all of the energy has been behind the achievement gap suffered by disadvantaged kids," he notes. "We've had to insist that as morally urgent as that is—and it is urgent—there has to be a broader-based strategy that draws political energies and public engagement from everywhere; otherwise, education reform won't succeed."

---

14. Interview 5/23/2013
15. Interview 5/23/2013

The Great Hearts Academies offer a "traditional American model" of education that integrates classroom work with extracurricular activities and athletics. The liberal arts curriculum is unusually rigorous, however. And an even more unusual essential element of the Great Hearts formula is the collective ethic the schools cultivate. Former teacher Dan Scoggin and his co-founders believed that surrounding students with "greatness"—great books, great human examples, tales of moral greatness—would help them feel their human value and potential.

"School culture is critical," says Heiler. The schools rely on a great books curriculum that substitutes classics for textbooks, Socratic-style discussions instead of lecturing, and teachers with in-depth subject expertise.

Great Hearts has no electives. All students take the same highly challenging sequence in math, science, foreign language, fine arts, and humanities. Students take Algebra I in seventh grade, which puts them all on path for calculus in eleventh and twelfth grade. Three years of Latin begin in sixth grade. Medieval history is required in eighth grade, and music and poetry in ninth and tenth. The "core reading list" for elementary students includes *Don Quixote, Gulliver's Travels, Treasure Island,* and *Narrative of the Life of Frederick Douglass.* For middle and high school, the list includes *The Aeneid, As I Lay Dying, Crime and Punishment, Federalist #10, Henry V, Plessy vs. Ferguson,* and *The Republic.*[16]

Clearly, the network's curriculum far exceeds state standards. And at the high-school level, 24.5 credits are required for graduation, considerably higher than the state's requirement of 20. Students graduate fully prepared for the rigors of the nation's top colleges and universities.

But Great Hearts also cares deeply about the moral formation of its students. GH teaches that genius is only fruitful for society if the individual is willing to work hard and act for the betterment of man. The academies seek to "graduate thoughtful leaders of character who will contribute to a more philosophical, humane, and just society."[17] Students wear uniforms and adhere to an honor code that includes fidelity to academic integrity. The schools try to instill nine core virtues in students: humility, integrity, friendship, perseverance, wisdom, courage, responsibility, honesty, and citizenship. One "philosophical pillar" of the network's culture is that "sarcasm, bad will, and apathy are toxic to the work of teaching and learning."[18]

---

16. Great Hearts Curriculum Overview, greatheartsaz.org/downloads/Curriculum%20Overview%201.23.13.pdf

17. Great Hearts School Model, greatheartsaz.org/index.php/school-model-sidemenu-37

18. Great Hearts Philosophical Pillars, greatheartsaz.org/index.php/philosophical-pillars

Great Hearts vigorously recruits instructors it believes will be exceptional classrooms leaders, regardless of their backgrounds or state certifications. "We place stock in content expertise and pedagogy, which don't necessarily track with teacher credentialing," states Heiler. (This topic will be further covered in Chapters 7 and 8.)

On 2012 statewide assessments, Great Hearts students outperformed the average Arizona student in every tested subject and every grade level.[19] Of the five schools with 2012 graduating classes, between 83 and 97 percent of graduating seniors were headed to four-year colleges. Fully 13 percent of all seniors at Chandler Prep., one of the network's high schools, were named National Merit Scholarhip Finalists.[20]

Examples like BASIS and Great Hearts make it clear that philanthropists don't have to invent something new, or pour money into unproven models, to help high-flying students. The ranks of high-achieving children can clearly be dramatically expanded, while each individual is pulled toward his highest level, just by applying lessons already learned. Certainly, expanding high-achievement schooling requires careful planning. Heiler points to "the premium on school leadership, which is a scarce resource in education in general," and notes that schools with high standards require "even greater faculty and administrative cohesion around school culture and discipline, and a bond of trust with the community so they buy in to what you're doing and support you."

Creating more schools capable of producing high achievers will also require more private philanthropic money. For instance, in Arizona as in many places, state reimbursements to charter schools are lower than reimbursements to conventional schools. One indicator during the launch of Great Hearts showed $7,806 government dollars going to every student in a charter school, versus $9,429 for students in conventional schools. So how are quality schools built on these pinched budgets? In most cases, it is philanthropy that bridges the gap. Local donors large and small—like the Quayle family who gave Great Hearts $1.5 million in 2012—have an essential role in making up the difference in ways that allow new-style schools to take off, particularly during the crucial start-up phases that all fledgling schools go through.

For philanthropists who understand the importance of reversing the last generation's neglect of high-potential students, there are many exciting opportunities today to create or support schools in the BASIS/Great

---

19. Great Hearts Quarterly Report, December 2012, greatheartsaz.org/downloads/DEC%20QR%202012.pdf
20. Ibid.

Hearts mold. "Philanthropists need to think strategically and find institutions they believe can be transformative," suggests Heiler. The educational status quo, which is now often so unfriendly to gifted students, will only improve, he argues, if philanthropists are "constructively disruptive in ways that compel change."

Though Great Hearts and BASIS are accomplishing remarkable feats for many students, neither—yet, at least—has completely cracked the code for bringing the most disadvantaged students up to the loftiest academic levels. On August 1, 2013, Arizona released letter grades for all of the state's schools; while most Great Hearts campuses received an A, Teleos Prep., their Phoenix campus serving a primarily low-income student body, received a C. Also, in the summer of 2013 BASIS's Washington school faced challenges adapting its model to special-education students. (Despite this, though, the campus attained D.C.'s "Reward" status, signifying its place among the city's highest performing schools, an almost unheard-of accomplishment for a school in its very first year.)[21]

BASIS relies on the extraordinary content knowledge of its teachers to ignite in students a passion and curiosity for learning—and to have the chops necessary to respond to the high-level questions of students.

Overcoming deep deprivation and pulling exceptional achievement out of middle-to-high-potential students are not the same task, and it is quite likely that different schools will be required for mastering each of those different undertakings. Philanthropists ought not expect every school to work with every population. Successful "No Excuses" charter schools have demonstrated that when they are provided with a wide array of additional supports, even seriously disadvantaged kids are capable of reaching the proficient level. Expecting them to hit exceptional performance may not always be realistic.

---

21. capitalcommunitynews.com/content/basis-meets-dc-public-charter-school-board

Options for high fliers within conventional districts: Exam schools

Some school districts meet the needs of academically talented students by operating selective public high schools, often referred to as "exam schools." These are not charter schools. They are not private schools. They are academically selective traditional public schools, "operated in more top-down fashion by districts, states, or sometimes universities rather than as freestanding and self-propelled institutions."[22]

At most exam schools students compete for admission based on their academic records. The schools then offer challenging classes, often including college coursework through partner colleges. Sometimes high-level opportunities are available outside the classroom, through independent projects or internships.[23] In short, exam schools can be thought of as "whole-school" versions of the "honors track" that often exists within a conventional high school.[24]

Alas, they are fairly rare. In their recent book *Exam Schools: Inside America's Most Selective Public High Schools*, authors Chester Finn and Jessica Hockett note that while there is ample demand for such schools, their numbers are small. It appears there are only about 165 across the nation.

Finn and Hockett conducted in-depth visits at 11 of the 165 exam schools they identified in their national search. While each school possessed a particular approach, culture, and environment, the authors noted that the schools they visited had a number of important commonalities. For one, "use of time—by day and by week—was structured in ways that facilitate in-depth learning and prepare students for a college schedule."[25] In exam schools, the amount of time dedicated to academics is much more akin to that of our global competitors. Journalist and fellow at the New America Foundation Amanda Ripley, who has been studying the education systems of leading nations, recently observed that "while the American school day can be as short as six hours, Korean kids attend school about eight or nine hours a day—and then many of them continue studying alone or with tutors until late into the night."[26]

---

22. Chester E. Finn and Jessica Hockett, *Exam Schools: Inside America's Most Selective Public High Schools*. Princeton University Press, 2012, pages 12-13

23. Chester E. Finn and Jessica Hockett, *Exam Schools: Inside America's Most Selective Public High Schools*. Princeton University Press, 2012, pages 12-13

24. Ibid., page 10

25. Ibid., page 160

26. Amanda Ripley, "Brilliance in a Box: What do the best classrooms in the world look like?" New America Foundation, October 20, 2010, newamerica.net/node/38764

Finn and Hockett found that all exam schools offered some form of college-level work, often for college credit, and a significantly advanced overall course of study: "At least some A.P. courses or the International Baccalaureate program—both of which are increasingly viewed as indicators of a school's academic rigor and quality."[27] Like the BASIS charter school described earlier, most exam schools don't just offer but *require* challenging classes led by expert educators and ultimately assessed by difficult end-of-year exams. These seem to be necessary conditions for pushing our most gifted students, and producing more of them: a slate of courses significantly more difficult than standard school fare, and teachers with absolute subject mastery.

There are, however, variations on the theme. The Davidson Academy in Reno, Nevada, for example, is a free public day school for profoundly gifted children (scoring in the 99.9th percentile on IQ tests). It requires rigorous study, but rather than building that around A.P. classes or other existing programs, it personalizes offerings for its specialized population of students. "We need to individualize their educations," argues Bob Davidson, the philanthropist behind the school. When it comes to the most gifted students, he insists, "cookie-cutter schools and classes can't serve these children well." Each student at Davidson Academy gets his own "Personalized Learning Plan" (akin to the "Individualized Education Program" that is required under federal law for a student with disabilities). At Davidson Academy, these flexible plans "serve as a roadmap for academic and personal goals."[28] A fascinating consequence of this approach is that students are grouped by ability rather than age or grade. This means that 12- and 16-year-olds may find themselves in some of the same classes if their learning plans overlap.

Entrance requirements

Often, note Finn and Hockett, the most controversial aspect of this kind of school is how children are selected for entry."[29] Every district, and even some schools within the same district, have their own set of criteria and process for admitting students: "The schools reported many different approaches, emphases, and criteria for admissions. A student's prior

---

27. Chester E. Finn and Jessica Hockett, *Exam Schools: Inside America's Most Selective Public High Schools,* Princeton University Press, 2012, page 54

28. "The Davidson Academy of Nevada: About the Davidson Academy of Nevada," davidsonacademy.unr. edu/Articles.aspx?ArticleID=173&NavID=6_9

29. Chester E. Finn and Jessica Hockett, *Exam Schools: Inside America's Most Selective Public High Schools,* Princeton University Press, 2012, page 162

academic performance is the most widely used criterion.... Applicants' scores on various tests also figure prominently. State- or district-administered tests appear to be the most widely considered.... Eighteen schools reported taking SAT or ACT scores into consideration, a dozen of them in a major way."[30]

Clearly there is little consensus among exam schools as to the best measures for evaluating and admitting students. Standardized tests continue to be prominent in many admissions algorithms. Many supplement them with other measures.

The most widely used supplements may be student essays and teacher recommendations. Some schools also use records of student behavior and attendance. "Several respondents described these criteria as evidence of a student's maturity or ability to assume greater responsibility in a more challenging or flexible academic setting," write Finn and Hockett. Other criteria used include the types and levels of courses previously taken, class rank, and the quality of previous schools attended. Many schools also consider race (with bonuses for minorities), income (with bonuses for the low-income), and whether the student would be the first in her family to attend college (with bonuses if so).[31]

Admissions procedures are inherently contentious for obvious reasons; some students are admitted and others are not. Given that nearly two thirds of exam schools reported to Finn and Hockett that they accepted fewer than half of their applicants, it appears that explicit and transparent acceptance criteria are essential for any public exam school's long-term sustainability.[32]

Philanthropists interested in building broader support for demanding, selective public schools might consider funding research on the most rational and fair systems for identifying students who could most benefit from such schools. Homogenization is certainly to be avoided, but the creation of "industry standards" might reduce some of the inherent controversy that makes selective schools controversial in some communities. Simply analyzing the admissions systems currently in place in public exam schools might be a good beginning; such a study could help build consensus behind reasonable, high-quality standards for selecting students. Certainly it is to be advised that donors deciding investing in programs for the gifted be cognizant of the selection systems the pro-

---

30. Ibid., page 39
31. Ibid., page 40
32. Ibid., page 42

gram will rely on. For the measures used on the front end will have a strong influence both on the eventual results in the schools, and on their standing among parents.

Community representation

Earlier in this volume, we looked at ideological struggles over admissions procedures used for gifted programs in New York City. While New York City's schools are more politicized than most, the controversies there can nonetheless be instructive of potential problems to be aware of when constructing schools that stretch high achievers. Perhaps most threatening is the fact that such schools, particularly in urban areas, often end up with less racial and ethnic diversity than their surrounding neighborhoods.

At the famous Stuyvesant High School in Lower Manhattan, for example, of the 3,295 students attending the school in 2012, only 40 were black, making up just over 1 percent of the student body. (African Americans make up 32 percent of all the students in New York City public schools.) Hispanic students, who make up about 40 percent of the city's public school students, occupy just 2 percent of Stuyvesant's seats.[33] Some experts say that racial "imbalance" (half or more of the students being of one race) is a problem in two thirds or more of exam schools.[34]

Finn and Hockett found that not one of the eleven schools they visited "was a demographic or socioeconomic miniature of the place it served." But they also found that the causes of this varied, and were generally benign in origin though not consequence. A school's location is one major factor: if located far from lower-income areas, simply getting to the school presents challenges to some students. Longer school days can make that situation worse—a 7 a.m. start and 5 p.m. dismissal become a serious disincentive if a student lives an hour or more from the campus. Poor elementary schools that leave students unprepared for high-level work, non-supportive families, lack of role-models for academic success, and many other factors can also make it hard for demanding schools to attract large numbers of poor and minority students.

But when the demographics of their student populations are at odds with the surrounding neighborhoods, particularly nearby traditional public schools, the challenges for academically selective schools are exacerbated.

---

33. Fernanda Santos, "To Be Black at Stuyvesant High," *New York Times*, February 25, 2012, nytimes. com/2012/02/26/education/black-at-stuyvesant-high-one-girls-experience.html?pagewanted=all&_r=0

34. Chester E. Finn and Jessica Hockett, "Exam Schools from the Inside," *Education Next*, Fall 2012, educationnext.org/exam-schools-from-the-inside

The old charges that such schools are elitist or, more provocatively, racist may rear their heads.

Many exam schools try to resolve this issue through their admissions processes. Jones College Prep, located in Chicago, was for 30 years required to follow a "racial balance" policy that dictated that the school's enrollment could not contain more than 30 percent of any one racial group. This court decree was vacated in 2009, returning control of the admissions process entirely to Chicago Public Schools administrators. Jones and other selective-admissions public schools in Chicago no longer explicitly use race as a criterion for entry. Instead, the district has adopted a complicated geographic selection policy.

Seventh graders hoping to attend Jones submit grades and standardized test scores and take an entrance exam. A rubric gives an applicant a certain number of points for each of those factors, and then applicants are ranked citywide. The top ranked students are offered seats until

> The vast majority of U.S. students have no access to a selective-admissions public school, no matter what their background or race or neighborhood.

30 percent of all available slots are filled. Then, to ensure diversity, the remaining 70 percent of seats are offered to applicants based on their scores relative to other students from their census tract within the city. While this policy is racially blind, it serves to maintain racial diversity in the city's selective schools, because neighborhoods are highly correlated to income and race.

This new policy, however, is not without controversy. One consequence is that students who live in wealthier parts of the city need a significantly higher academic score than those living in low-income areas. Nevertheless, the principal of Jones argues that this new admissions system is working. All of Chicago's nine selective-admissions schools have a white population of less than 40 percent today, and four selective schools in the heavily black school district have African-American populations above 75 percent.[35]

---

35. Ibid., pages 101-102

The admissions process for Townsend Harris High School, located in Queens, New York, relies on a complex citywide high-school matching system. All eighth graders in New York City pass through a centralized system before attending ninth grade (unless they enroll in a charter, private, or parochial school). Selective-admissions schools like Townsend Harris establish their own admissions prerequisites and then rank applicants that come from the centralized system based on those criteria. A complicated algorithm matches student to program, based on each party's preferences.

In addition to this system, the city operates a special admissions process for nine of its most competitive high schools, based solely on student test scores on the Specialized High Schools Admissions Test. Students can apply to both the test-based schools and the traditional high-school programs. The student body that ends up enrolled at Townsend Harris is a mix of both—test-selected students coupled with "zone" quotas within Queens to ensure that Townsend doesn't skim only top students.

In the end, these systems have resulted in the following demographic profile: Within New York City's 23 selective high schools, 51 percent of all students are Asian, 27 percent are white, 12 percent are Hispanic, 6 percent are black, and 4 percent are multiracial.[36] This still does not match the city's overall student composition, but it give heavy weight to the personal preferences of the city's students while also attempting to accurately locate higher-potential students.

Three time zones away in California, other schools are employing similarly byzantine school-selection mechanisms. Oxford Academy in Orange County has a complicated weighting mechanism akin to that used in Chicago Public Schools. After students meet minimum grade and standardized test scores, applicants take a four-hour entrance exam. The top 25 scorers from each junior high are rank ordered, and then the students' scores are weighted according to the neighborhood they come from. In this way, approximately 200 seventh-grade openings are distributed.[37]

On average, exam schools enroll about the same percentage of low-income youngsters as public secondary schools generally, but these schools are often located in inner cities, where poverty rates are higher than that. Finn and Hockett note that there are many factors which can separate children from high-expectation schools: "For these schools to be

36. Ibid., pages 115-117
37. Ibid., page 135

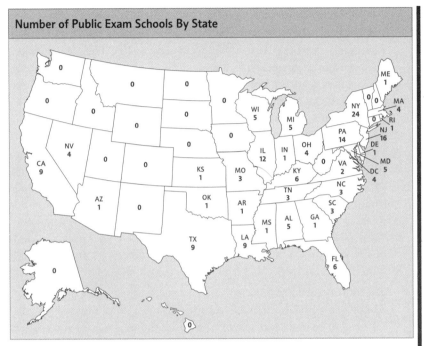

Number of Public Exam Schools By State

Source: Finn and Hockett study, educationnext.org/exam-schools-from-the-inside

realistic options for children, parents need sufficient means to transport their youngsters across town each day—and must *not* need them urgently to earn money, learn a useful trade, or help around the house. Moreover, to qualify for supercharged high schools, students must generally attend solid primary and junior high schools. It also helps if their homes and neighborhoods are amply supplied with books, periodicals, and intellectually active people."[38]

Increasing the supply of demanding schools

The very biggest impediment to accessibility, however, has nothing to do with family life or admissions or poverty. The most momentous, and sad, barrier is just that there are too few of these schools focusing on high-potential scholars in existence. The vast majority of U.S. students have no access to a selective-admissions public school, no matter what their background or race or neighborhood. There are a number of states that have zero academically selective public high schools. In most states the grand total is in the single digits.

---

38. Ibid., page 14

Because of shortsighted policies and resistance from ideologues, the supply of exam schools doesn't come close to meeting the demand today. The map nearby lists the public exam schools that Finn and Hockett uncovered in their research. Obviously, there is great need for a strategy to plant new academically selective institutions within public school districts across the U.S.

Philanthropists could take a number of steps to ensure that more of these schools are created in the years to come. First, they should help ensure that state policy doesn't erect insurmountable impediments to selective-admission public schools. If state statute does prohibit such schools, an information and advocacy campaign is needed. Those policies must be changed.

Where such schools are already allowable, a donor could partner with the state department of education, a school district, or an institution of higher education to create new institutions. Selective schools can take many forms—focusing on math and technology, for instance, or fine arts, or literature, or entrepreneurship. A particular focus can, among other things, help a philanthropist find partners such as local museums or laboratories or businesses that will help create the new school and support it once open.

Donors might also consider investing in existing schools. This could take the form of facilitating their growth—expanding a school to serve more students by adding enrollment or new grades, or replicating its model on additional campuses elsewhere. Other means of support could include adding new programs within a school (adding an engineering curriculum at a science-oriented school, or offering visual arts at a music-focused school. Donors could also just help an existing school to recruit and retain highly effective educators, start an endowment for the school, or take other measures to ensure that the facility meets its professed goal of pulling the very best work out of its precocious students.

Donors also have options outside of traditional school districts. There are, of course, countless private schools that cater to high-achieving kids. In many regions private schools are the lifeline and sole recourse for gifted children who would otherwise languish in mediocre public schools. Nearly all private schools try to keep costs from keeping bright children out, and donors can help with this by endowing scholarship funds or simply bolstering the school in other ways.

There are also budding efforts today to develop new models of private schools. Among the more well known is Avenues, the "world school." Founded and run by serial education entrepreneur Chris Whittle, Avenues seeks to become "one international school with 20 or more campuses." The first campus opened in New York City in the fall of 2012 with 750 students in pre-K through ninth grade.[39] There are also many promising efforts to build effective new private schools around "blended learning" methods, which mesh online instruction with in-person tutoring.[40] Funders may find that the freedoms afforded by operating outside of the public sector make it easier to apply fresh approaches and pursue rapid improvement and growth.

When it comes to charter schools, most state laws require them to be open admission—meaning that exam schools and other forms of selecting students by potential cannot exist in the charter sector for the most part. There is substantial political value in maintaining this feature of chartering (it is one of the strongest defenses against antagonists who attack the charter as "unfair" and "elitist"). And as examples like the BASIS and Great Hearts schools demonstrate clearly, it is possible even at open-admission schools to create demanding schools where high-potential students are pushed and pulled to excellence along with others.

Nonetheless, good arguments for allowing selective-admissions charters can be made. The first is that the freedoms afforded charters so greatly facilitate the startup of new schools that it is unwise to close this sector to social entrepreneurs hoping to serve neglected high-potential students. Charters offer the flexibility to swiftly get high-quality schools off the ground and serving students, particularly underprivileged ones, who are now languishing in conventional schools.

Second, chartering is especially good at enabling great schools to replicate themselves and expand rapidly, as high-flying charter-school networks like KIPP (141 campuses nationwide), Aspire (37 schools), Uncommon Schools (32), IDEA Public Schools (28), Achievement First (22), Success Academy (20), and YES Prep (11) have demonstrated. Craig Barrett, the former Intel executive whose philanthropy helped expand the BASIS charter network, explained in an interview that much of the success of replications in the charter sector can be attributed to charters being insulated from the traditional school system and its many enervating policies and habits.[41]

39. "Avenues: The World School," avenues.org

40. Laura Vanderkam, *Blended Learning: A Wise Giver's Guide to Supporting Tech-assisted Teaching*, The Philanthropy Roundtable, 2013

41. Interview 4/30/2013

Third, charters' freedom (in some states) from regulations related to teacher credentialing would be invaluable to exam-style schools. Teachers of exceptionally bright students need to be exceptionally knowledgeable in particular subject areas, and being able to hire young Ph.D.s, retired engineers, performing musicians, former technologists, ex-military leaders, and experienced business executives even if they are non-certified, instead of just relying on graduates of teacher colleges, could be enormously valuable. Experiments at charters in finding non-conventional yet highly effective teachers could offer lessons that might eventually be applied at conventional schools as well.

Opening the door to selective-admissions charters would require legislative action in most states. Donors intrigued by the idea may consider working with their state charter-school associations and other education-reform advocacy groups to explore the possibilities.

Charter schools that would cater to truly gifted students are not currently allowed under most state charter laws, and districts typically only have magnet programs at the high school level—meaning that nine years of a high-potential student's education are sub-optimal. Never before has our nation done so little to cultivate exceptional children.

There are already a few extant examples of charter schools dedicated to gifted students. These may provide some direction to funders considering this path.

The Metrolina Regional Scholars Academy of Charlotte, North Carolina, which was founded in 2000, serves 360 students in grades K-eighth. To be eligible, a student must score three standard deviations above the mean on an IQ test (145 or above); 13 out of every 10,000 individuals achieve such a score. The school believes that gifted students require schooling different than "standard classroom activities." "They learn more rapidly...need time for in-depth exploration and investigation, and ask challenging questions." Accordingly, Metrolina has a rigorous curriculum and highly educated teachers, and provides its students with the "ability to interact with their same aged peers with similar intellect."[42]

A subtle clause in North Carolina's charter law makes Metrolina—an exam-style charter school—possible in the state. If the school's mission is to focus on a particular group of students, state law stipulates, and these details are made explicit in its charter agreement, and an authorizer approves its application, then the school may have entrance criteria. Ohio is another state with a statute allowing for such exam-style charter schools. We'll look at an interesting institution in that state next.

Case study: Menlo Park Academy

There were 368 charter schools open during the 2011-2012 school year in the state of Ohio. Of these schools, 26 were online schools, 87 were dropout-recovery schools, and 35 were dedicated to the needs of students with disabilities. One, Menlo Park Academy, stands out as the state's only charter school for gifted and talented students.[43]

Ohio has a state definition of gifted and talented, which includes "specific academic ability," "creative thinking ability," and "visual or performing arts ability."[44] Districts are required to identify gifted students. Bewilderingly, though, they are not required to serve these students once identified. It is thus estimated that of Ohio's 265,555 gifted-identified students, only about 18 percent actually receive any targeted services.[45]

Cleverly utilizing the provision of Ohio's charter law allowing a charter to limit its enrollment to a defined set of "at-risk" students, Menlo Park Academy seeks to provide high-potential Ohio students with the specific supports they need to flourish.[46] Located in southwest Cleveland, the school serves more than 300 students drawn from 40 school

---

42. "Metrolinia Regional Scholars Academy," scholarsacademy.org

43. Aaron Churchill, "Charters for the gifted and talented?" *Thomas B. Fordham Institute Ohio Gadfly Daily*, March 21, 2013, edexcellence.net/commentary/education-gadfly-daily/ohio-gadfly-daily/2013/charters-for-the-gifted-and-talented.html

44. Ohio Revised Code 3324.03, codes.ohio.gov/orc/3324.03

45. Ellen Belcher, "A school for the gifted: Menlo Park Academy," *Thomas B. Fordham Institute Ohio Gadfly Daily*, May 29, 2013, edexcellence.net/ohio-policy/gadfly/2013/may-29/a-school-for-the-gifted-menlo-park-academy.html

46. Ohio Revised Code 3314.06 codes.ohio.gov/orc/3314.06

districts in and around the city.[47] Admitted students must fall in the top 5 percent of their age group (an IQ of 127) or meet another state standard qualifying them as gifted. The school gives admissions preference to gifted students living in Cleveland proper, and to the qualifying siblings of existing students.

Menlo Park has experienced rapid growth after beginning with barely more than three dozen students in 2008—demonstrating the demand for such a school. Because of over-enrollment, the school had to establish a lottery beginning in the 2012-2013 school year. Currently there are 46 students on the waiting list, 22 of them for a spot in the accelerated kindergarten program.[48]

Students are first placed in traditional grade clusters, with two classes in each early grade (K-third). Older students (fourth-eighth grades) are less rigidly assigned, often taking classes with younger and older students depending on their specific abilities in each subject. Despite its popularity, the school has challenges. It currently leases space in a former Catholic school, and the roof leaks, there are no gas lines in the science rooms for experiments, and overcrowding has pushed students into modular units.

With so many families seeking its services, Menlo Park's future appears strong. Yet it requires significant outside support. In Ohio, like most states, the state doesn't reimburse charter schools as generously as conventional public schools. Menlo Park administrators say that government funds cover only 65 percent of its costs, and as a charter school it cannot charge tuition.[49]

As Menlo Park demonstrates, donors interested in charter schools focused on high-achievers have many options available to them. Keeping the embryonic schools in this sector open and flourishing is one possible service. Helping such schools expand or replicate would also be valuable. And there are vast opportunities for developing entirely new models of selective- admission charter schools.

Tom Torkelson, founder of IDEA Public Schools, one of the nation's finest (and largest) charter operators, talked to us about the intersection of gifted education, disadvantaged kids, and selective admissions. "There

47. Aaron Churchill, "Charters for the gifted and talented?" *Thomas B. Fordham Institute Ohio Gadfly Daily*, March 21, 2013, edexcellence.net/commentary/education-gadfly-daily/ohio-gadfly-daily/2013/charters-for-the-gifted-and-talented.html

48. Ellen Belcher, "A school for the gifted: Menlo Park Academy." *Thomas B. Fordham Institute Ohio Gadfly Daily.* May 29, 2013. edexcellence.net/ohio-policy/gadfly/2013/may-29/a-school-for-the-gifted-menlo-park-academy.html

49. "Menlo Park Academy," menloparkacademy.com/support-mpa

has been an important focus over the last decade on two achievement gaps—the one within the U.S. between middle-income and low-income students, and the one between the U.S. and every other industrialized nation. What's been missing from the policy debate is how to help exceptionally gifted students reach their fullest potential," said Torkelson.

"In our system of high-performing charter schools we celebrate a student who scores a perfect score on, say, a fifth-grade state math test. But what we often don't realize is that that child might also have scored perfectly on a high school math test if the system was flexible enough to allow him to accelerate to that level. Charter schools that would cater to truly gifted students are not currently allowed under most state charter laws, and districts typically only have magnet programs at the high-school level—meaning that nine years of a high-potential student's education are sub-optimal. Never before has our nation done so little to cultivate genuinely exceptional children."

Reasons for donor support

In all segments of gifted education, and especially selective schools, there is great need for new thinking about student recruitment, selection, and retention. Donors might help an existing high school do a better job of locating high-potential students. They might help schools become more representative of their wider community (for instance, by guaranteeing some number of seats to students in every sending junior high, improving marketing in low-income neighborhoods, or ensuring transportation options for those in need).

Philanthropists more interested in pairing as many students as possible with schools that maximize their potential could partner with institutions of higher education to develop new systems for capturing students' abilities and preferences and then matching them with institutions. When the school districts of New York City and Boston decided to give families more choices in high schools for their kids, they partnered with economists at Harvard, Columbia, and Duke, to craft sophisticated algorithms for offering enrollment options.[50]

Of course, better sifting and sorting only redistributes existing seats; it does nothing to bring opportunities to additional children. But donors in areas where these schools do exist should be mindful of the many pressures they are under. While we try to grow more, we need to protect

---

50. Thomas Toch and Chad Aldeman, "Matchmaking: Enabling mandatory public school choice in New York and Boston," *Education Sector*, September 2009

the ones that we have. Despite the widespread perception that they are "privileged" and have resources to burn, many of today's schools serving high-potential children are in a precarious position. They are often the first victims of belt-tightening when school districts and state governments face cash shortages. Finn and Hockett, for instance, report that all of the public exam schools they studied face "pressures that could eventually alter them, perhaps even threaten their existence."[51]

When budget cuts force these schools to reduce their staffs and slash extracurricular activities, private funding can help. Strategic donors can support teaching positions and protect important programs. Thomas Jefferson High School, an academically selective public school located in Fairfax County, Virginia, which has been ranked the No. 1 high school in America by *U.S. News and World Report*, has been able to raise a substantial amount of private funding. The school has created its own subsidiary non-profit organization called the Thomas Jefferson Partnership Fund, which now annually provides up to $700,000 of highly flexible enrichment funding. Donors include alumni, parents, and corporations.[52]

The existing specialty schools serving gifted students are invaluable. Their place on the K-12 landscape must be kept secure; in the future their footprint must expand. Even if the vast majority of high-potential students will always be served by boutique programs within larger comprehensive schools, having a critical mass of entire schools that are focused solely on gifted students is vital, as testing grounds and proofs of need and value. These schools also serve as training grounds for great teachers, and offer lofty examples toward which ambitious principals, teachers, and students elsewhere can strive.

As experts put it, unusually talented students "benefit when the entire team pulls in the same direction." Small specialty programs embedded within much larger schools can be completely excised when budgets get tight; they may need to defend their *raison d'êtres* to every new principal, new superintendent, or new slate of school board members. They (and their students) may suffer accusations of elitism, or feel pressured to water down their offerings.

Specialized schools are also able to develop a depth of curricular choices, top-level instructional offerings, community and alumnae sup-

51. Chester E. Finn and Jessica Hockett, *Exam Schools: Inside America's Most Selective Public High Schools*, Princeton University Press, 2012, page 165

52. Ibid., page 158

ports, counseling services, and financial resources that no boutique offering has the luxury of possessing. When you go from a high-achiever program to a high-achiever school, you feel the difference, and realize the important advantages of scale.

Finally, such schools can have a lasting influence that extends far beyond their current classes and alumni. They are able to build proud reputations that can draw families to a region, change neighborhoods, and spur economic development. Many exam schools are regional gems and act as magnets for underserved children from far afield. This makes them sources of local pride, and major attractions for other strivers.[53]

Mark Gleason is executive director of the Philadelphia Schools Partnership, which is raising $100 million for "The Great Schools Fund"—an effort to create 35,000 seats in high-performing schools in the City of Brotherly Love. Lead Investors in the fund include the William Penn Foundation, the Maguire Family Foundation, and Janine and Jeff Yass. "In Philadelphia we are focused on ensuring there are great schools available to every child—and to every type of child," says Gleason. "There is no model that can serve every student. A great educational system must provide a variety of options so that all types of student can be challenged and developed. Properly serving the most gifted students is every bit as important as serving the most struggling students. But we must also be wary not to define "gifted" in ways that don't spot those students who are both gifted and disadvantaged."

---

53. Ibid., pages 198-199

> ### Summary of Investment Possibilities

- Identify promising enrichment programs (like the Schoolwide Enrichment Model) and support them by offering a school funding for staff, training, or supplies
- Cover startup costs for new charter and private schools committed to extraordinarily high expectations
- Support the expansion and replication of superb schools like BASIS and Great Hearts
- Fund the dissemination of best practices from schools succeeding with high-performing students, so other schools can learn
- Support research on how best to advance low-income kids into high-achievers
- Invest in advocacy campaigns to create more selective-admissions traditional public schools
- Support efforts to ensure fair representation of low-income and minority students in exam schools
- Invest in advocacy campaigns to alter charter laws to allow a focus on gifted students
- Fund charter-school incubators willing to launch gifted-focused schools

Traditional School-based Initiatives

Unfortunately, academically selective schools have only a tiny foothold within U.S. public education today. Of the more than 22,000 public high schools in the United States, for instance, there are less than 200 that purposefully pull together high-potential students. "Public education has seldom opted for the 'whole school' approach to address the distinctive needs of high-performing and high-potential youngsters," note Finn and Hockett. "Far more often, it has opted for programs, courses, and tracks—often just as selective, but less overt about it—within schools that, at least on the surface, are accessible to everyone."[1]

---

1. Ibid., page 172

Offering exceptionally bright children in-school extras allows existing schools to keep their top students (and claim their test scores and accomplishments), while the kids get a bit of added attention. There are scads of ways this tends to be done, but most variations can be categorized into one of three groups: Acceleration. High-level content specialization (e.g. STEM or the arts). Or online and other technological learning supplements.

These options (and the many others out there) differ in numerous ways. When done well, though, they share a common characteristic: They enable high-capacity kids to undertake more challenging work that keeps them engaged and pushes them to greater levels of achievement.

It is at the extreme ends of the performance spectrum where students require the greatest degree of personalized instruction. Boys and girls with academic disabilities are now provided with elaborately individualized and heavily resourced education programs. Advanced students lack similar accommodation to work at their natural rate of learning.

Acceleration

Acceleration may be the easiest and most cost-effective way to give gifted students continuous access to more challenging material. It allows them to remain in their traditional neighborhood schools and traditional classrooms, yet enables them to grapple with content—and peers—more closely aligned with their above-age academic capabilities. Acceleration allows a student to bypass units, courses, or entire grade levels so that the pace of instruction and complexity of curriculum better match the student's readiness and motivation to learn.[2]

The commonest methods of acceleration include early admission to kindergarten for especially precocious youngsters; grade skipping for stu-

2. Nicholas Colangelo, Susan G. Assouline, and Miraca U. M. Gross, *A Nation Deceived: How Schools Hold Back America's Brightest Students*, Volume I, October 2004

dents excelling across the board; advancing to a higher grade in a specific subject area for a student with a particular gift; early high school graduation for students prepared for college work; and concurrent enrollment in college for students who would benefit from both the high school experience and college-level material.[3]

Allowing academically advanced students the opportunity to accelerate through content they have already mastered immediately provides them with more difficult material. This helps them keep growing mentally, and reduces academic "coasting." It is important to continuously challenge and place fresh demands on highly able students, otherwise they may never learn invaluable skills like perseverance that are acquired by struggling through difficult assignments.[4]

The 2004 research report *A Nation Deceived* argues that acceleration is in many ways an original component of America's public education system, dating back to one-room schoolhouse days where individual students by necessity learned at their own paces, sometimes mingled with older students, sometimes with younger, according to ability and content mastery, not age. Children moved through the curricula as quickly as they could or as slowly as necessary.[5]

When America's rapid growth in population led to the replacement of one-room schoolhouses with more standardized schools, students were grouped according to age instead of by ability and motivation. "This was not an educational decision," notes *A Nation Deceived*. "It was an organizational decision based upon a narrow understanding of child and adolescent development that supported the goal of keeping kids with their age-mates.... What was lost was an appreciation for individual differences."[6]

Of course, good teaching will be as important as accelerated curriculum. It is at the extremes—the ends of the student performance distribution—where individual differences are the most pronounced and where students require the greatest degree of personalized instruction. Our schools and public policies have recognized this for years when it comes to the left side of the distribution. Boys and girls with academic disabilities are now provided with elaborately individualized and heavily resourced education programs.

---

3. Nancy W. Toth, "Gifted Education: A Critical Discussion," March 1999, eric.ed.gov.proxygw.wrlc.org/PDFS/ED430331.pdf

4. Ibid.

5. Nicholas Colangelo, Susan G. Assouline, and Miraca U. M. Gross. *A Nation Deceived: How Schools Hold Back America's Brightest Students*, Volume I. October 2004

6. Ibid., page 11

However, advanced students—those represented by the tail on the right side of the distribution—lack similar attention to their needs. They are seldom given the opportunity to progress at their natural rates of learning, and seldom offered special instruction. Instead, they are held back, forced to learn at a common, standardized pace set by policies and practices that unfortunately elevate age above ability.[7]

Acceleration isn't just academically sensible; it is also a relatively easy, low-cost (and in some cases cost-*saving*) intervention. Moving students up a grade level, for a single course or all courses, does not require the hiring of any additional or specialized teachers or the creation or implementation of new curricula. There can also be economies for the family: students who pass A.P. tests can earn college credit, thereby saving money and time that would otherwise be spent on college.

In an era of tight school and family budgets these are significant benefits. Any intervention that both saves money and meets the needs of an important group of students ought to be embraced. It is certainly a strategy that philanthropists could emphasize in their attempts to inform policymakers about the needs of gifted students and practices that can serve them best.

If you are assuming that acceleration already is widely practiced, you sadly are mistaken. Many teachers and parents fear that acceleration will leave gaps in a child's content knowledge, or worse, hurry them through childhood, surround them with peers with whom they are out of step, and make it difficult for them to adjust socially.[8] History, however, suggests that acceleration can solve emotional problems as well, and it demonstrates that many successful public figures moved through school at an accelerated pace:

- Supreme Court Justice Sandra Day O'Connor graduated from high school at 16.
- Martin Luther King Jr. graduated from high school at age 15.
- Poet T. S. Eliot finished his undergraduate degree at Harvard in three years, his master's degree in one year.
- Writer Eudora Welty enrolled in college at age 16.
- Molecular biologist Joshua Lederberg graduated high school at 15, and went on to become the youngest recipient of the Nobel Prize at 33.

---

7. Ibid.
8. Ibid.

- Scientist James Watson earned his bachelor's degree at age 19 and his Ph.D. at 22, then made pioneering studies of DNA.[9]

These individuals did enormous good for our country and the world. Accelerating them through school certainly was in their best interests; it kept them challenged, and enabled them to learn more and more. It was also in the public's interest: "When great leaders reach society early, everyone benefits," argue experts on this subject.[10]

Despite the research pointing to the benefits of academic acceleration for gifted learners, many states and districts have no clear policies on the matter. Only eight states have policies that specifically permit acceleration, while 12 states have policies that allow districts to determine whether acceleration is permitted or not. Many districts frown upon early admittance to kindergarten, for example.[11]

James Borland, a professor at Columbia University Teachers College, writes that "acceleration is one of the most curious phenomena in the field of education. I can think of no other issue in which there is such a gulf between what research has revealed and what most practitioners believe. The research on acceleration is so uniformly positive, the benefits of appropriate acceleration so unequivocal, that it is difficult to see how an educator could oppose it."[12]

Given this clear research verdict, philanthropists interested in supporting acceleration should gather a full understanding of the policies in their target state or district. Helping parents and students advocate for better, clearer policies and practices may be useful. Then raising awareness, disseminating research, and informing families of their options could be highly beneficial.

Enhancing science, technology, engineering, and math (STEM)

It is now widely accepted that trends in the economy and international landscape make high-quality science, technology, engineering, and math education crucial to the future success of countries. Investing in high-quality STEM schools and programs is one way for philanthropists

---

9. Ibid.

10. Ibid., page 13

11. Nicholas Colangelo, Susan G. Assouline, and Miraca U. M. Gross, *A Nation Deceived: How Schools Hold Back America's Brightest Students*, Volume I, October 2004

12. Ibid., page 16

to develop a deeper pool of academically talented youth with the skills needed to succeed in tomorrow's workplace. It is also an investment in sustaining our country's global competitiveness.

Jim Rahn, president of the Kern Family Foundation, which invests significantly in STEM activities, believes we are "living in a world that is STEM-centric. Not just students who will pursue STEM-focused careers, but *all* students need more STEM literacy, because so many huge economic fields like health care, environmental remediation, and information technology have STEM orientations. We need to educate the next generation to be STEM-literate so we can have meaningful policy debates on these important issues."[13]

High-profile national reports echo this argument. The 2005 National Academies' report *Rising Above the Gathering Storm* posited that STEM leadership would be essential for creating the innovations necessary to

> All students need a more robust experience in STEM literacy, not just those who will pursue STEM-focused careers.

sustain America's future prosperity. The 2009 report *Strategy for American Innovation* agreed.[14] A 2010 report from the National Science Board warned that "to ensure the long-term prosperity of our nation, we must renew our collective commitment to excellence in education and the development of scientific talent.... The nation needs STEM innovators—those individuals who have developed the expertise to become leading STEM professionals and perhaps the creators of significant breakthroughs or advances in scientific and technological understanding."[15] As things currently stand, the board concluded, we're not up to the task:"The U.S. education system too frequently fails to identify and develop our most talented and motivated students who will become the next generation of innovators."[16]

---

13. Interview

14. National Science Board, "Preparing the Next Generation of STEM Innovators: Identifying and Developing our Nation's Human Capital," May 2010, nagc.org/uploadedFiles/Information_and_Resources/Hot_Topics/NSB%20-%20Stem%20innovators.pdf

15. Ibid.

16. Ibid.

U.S. math scores on the international PISA test have lagged behind those of our peers in the developed world and have even fallen below many lesser-developed countries. In the 2009 assessment, the U.S. average score of 487 was below the developed-nation average of 496, leaving us lower than 17 other industrial countries.[17] In science, the 2009 U.S. average lagged 12 other industrial nations.[18]

Further, there is evidence that the top-performing U.S. students, possibly because of our lagging STEM education, are eschewing careers in science and engineering. A 2002 analysis showed that between 1992 and 2000, the number of high-achieving students intending to enter graduate study in STEM fields declined 8 percent overall, with the largest declines in engineering (25 percent) and mathematics (19 percent).[19] As a result, many of these fields are becoming heavily reliant on foreign-born talent.

More troubling indicators:

- U.S. undergraduate students chose natural science and engineering as their primary field of study at considerably lower rates than in competing countries: 16 percent in the U.S., versus 25 percent in the European Union, 47 percent in China, and 38 percent in South Korea.[20]
- Further along the STEM pipeline, foreigners on temporary visas now earn 57 percent of all U.S. engineering doctorates, 54 percent of all computer science doctorates, and 51 percent of physics doctoral degrees.[21]
- In 2008, about 5 million science and engineering university degrees were awarded worldwide; students in the European Union earned 19 percent, students in the United States earned only 10 percent.[22]
- The global research force in science and engineering tripled from 1995 to 2007, but grew only from one million to 1.5 million in the U.S.[23]

17. National Center for Education Statistics, "Highlights from PISA 2009," December 2010, nces.ed.gov/pubs2011/2011004.pdf

18. Ibid.

19. National Science Board, "Preparing the Next Generation of STEM Innovators: Identifying and Developing our Nation's Human Capital," May 2010, nagc.org/uploadedFiles/Information_and_Resources/Hot_Topics/NSB%20-%20Stem%20innovators.pdf

20. Ibid.

21. Ibid.

22. Ibid.

23. Ibid.

If we believe STEM fields will produce many of our future jobs and drive much of our future economic growth, clearly we have a lot of work to do. Improved and expanded science education for our top students should be a big part of our strategy. Alas, able youngsters with interest frequently lack the opportunities they need to build STEM mastery today.

In its 2010 report, the National Science Board made some important recommendations for advancing STEM education: Provide opportunities for excellence via curriculum acceleration and enrichment, including expanding access among high school students to college-level and dual enrollment programs. Make sure that STEM teachers undergo rigorous, research-based, content-specific preparation. Districts and schools should develop partnerships between higher education institutions, museums, industry, and research laboratories, and K-12 schools to locate teaching talent. Schools, districts, and states must be held accountable for the performance of their very top students.[24]

The door is wide open for philanthropists willing to invest in STEM-focused schools and programs. The demand is so broad that donors will have opportunities to choose partners and follow their own interests. Some examples of possible initiatives:

- Develop internship partnerships linking top students with local universities, research labs, museums, or industries.
- Work with the state or local districts to create a Master Teacher Corps that attracts and develops excellent STEM teachers, including from unconventional sources like retirees, ex-military, former business technologists.
- Support demanding after-school and summer programs for students.
- Underwrite high-quality STEM enrichment programs in disadvantaged schools and neighborhoods.
- Support special STEM schools; for instance, philanthropist John Malone (who is an engineer, the son of an engineer, and the donor of engineering buildings at Yale and Johns Hopkins) provided $7 million to the Denver School of Science and Technology between 2011 and 2013 to expand that acclaimed

---

24. National Science Board, "Preparing the Next Generation of STEM Innovators: Identifying and Developing our Nation's Human Capital," May 2010, nagc.org/uploadedFiles/Information_and_Resources/Hot_Topics/NSB%20-%20Stem%20innovators.pdf

grades 6-12 charter school from five schools serving 1,500 students to ten schools that will marinate 4,500 students in mathematics, engineering, and science on the way to their high school degree.

There are countless philanthropic initiatives already under way in STEM education. The section following profiles three major national efforts by donors. These will give a sense of the enormous influence that smart investments can make.

Project Lead the Way, 100Kin10, and NMSI

Project Lead the Way (PLTW) provides rigorous and innovative STEM education to more than 500,000 middle school and high school students in over 5,000 schools across the country.[25] Its comprehensive curriculum for engineering and biomedical sciences "has been collaboratively designed by PLTW teachers, university educators, engineering and biomedical professionals, and school administrators to promote critical thinking, creativity, innovation, and real-world problem solving skills in students."[26]

In addition to providing a demanding top-notch curriculum, PLTW makes sure that the teachers running its programs are highly knowledgeable, trained, and effective. (Many of today's science teachers in public schools did not major in the sciences in college; that is a big part of our problem today.) Prior to leading a PLTW course, a teacher must complete a two-week, 80-hour training course at one of PTLW's affiliate universities. These courses are team-taught by university professors and PLTW master teachers. Because of the priority the program places on subject-matter expertise, those teaching multiple PTLW courses at the high school level must complete a separate training course for each subject taught.

The Kern Family Foundation is "zealous" in its support of PLTW. Unlike other "project-based" programs that may be interesting to students but lack academic rigor, PLTW is known for a curriculum that is both deeply engaging and highly challenging academically. "It has rigor and relevance unlike any other program I've seen," says Jim Rahn, Kern president. "Suddenly students start seeing the value in knowing and understanding the quadratic equation."

25. Interview 6/7/2013
26. "Project Lead the Way," pltw.org/about-us/who-we-are

Universities and corporations see the value of PLTW as well: 35 percent of incoming engineering majors at the University of Minnesota were PLTW graduates; 38 percent of incoming engineering majors at the Milwaukee School of Engineering were PLTW graduates. Indeed, products of the program receive several thousands of dollars in additional scholarship funding at some colleges just for having completed the curriculum.[27] Companies like Toyota, eager for employees with high degrees of technical training, similarly embrace PLTW graduates. PLTW has a wide array of corporate partners (including 3M, Cargill, Chevron, Intel, John Deere, Lockheed Martin, and Northrup Grumman) and numerous philanthropic backers in addition to the Kern Family Foundation, including the Ewing Marion Kauffman Foundation and the John S. and James L. Knight Foundation.

A wide array of dedicated schools focus on high-level arts education, out of recognition that gifted young artists need rigorous training if they are to be prepared for the intense competition they'll face in conservatories and the professional arts world.

Another approach can be seen in the audacious ambitions of the "100Kin10" program. Launched in 2011, this initiative seeks to train and retain 100,000 highly effective science, technology, engineering, and math teachers by 2021. The ultimate goal is to ensure that "all students have access to first-rate STEM learning so we can reverse our nation's decades-long decline in math and science."[28]

The project traces its pedigree to a January 2011 meeting of numerous STEM-related organizations convened by the Carnegie Corporation of New York (one of the nation's biggest philanthropies) and the Opportunity Equation (a math and science initiative). Officially announced at a Clinton Global Initiative that summer, 100Kin10 quickly gathered a wide array of partners, now numbering more than 150. Cooperating parties include government bodies, non-profits, corporations, universities,

---

27. Interview 6/7/2013
28. "100Kin10," 100kin10.org/page/goal-vision

foundations, and more. Participants commit to take efforts to increased the supply of STEM educators, develop and retain them, and build the larger movement. The University of Chicago Urban Education Institute and Center for Elementary Mathematics and Science Education play a key role in ensuring that partners focus on quality not just quantity. A process is being developed to regularly review the rigor of participating programs, provide guidance and support, and broadly share best practices.

The organization has started by convening meetings where successful ideas can be shared, by encouraging collaboration among schools, and by launching research. A $200,000 competition will "identify and build evidence for promising interventions, solutions, and treatments to prepare, support, develop, and retain the next generation of excellent STEM teachers."

Funders who care to support 100Kin10 commit a minimum of $500,000 over three years to support project partners. Partners are able to apply to all donors through a single common application form, but donors "maintain total independence of decision-making in choosing which organizations to fund." With its second fund now closed, 100Kin10 has so far raised a total of $52 million from 26 givers including Google, the Dow Chemical and Amgen foundations, the Boston Foundation, the Bill & Melinda Gates Foundation, the Michael & Susan Dell Foundation, the William and Flora Hewlett Foundation, and the John D. and Catherine T. MacArthur Foundation.[29] To date, 79 grants totaling $27,730,811 have been made to 41 partners. The initiative says it is on pace to produce 41,685 STEM educators by 2016.

The National Math + Science Initiative (NMSI) was created to address the declining number of students prepared to take rigorous post-secondary math and science courses. It seeks to improve student performance in STEM subjects by improving teaching and raising the quality of STEM curricula. Its financial supporters include the Bill & Melinda Gates Foundation, the ExxonMobil Corp., and the Michael & Susan Dell Foundation.

Rather than launching new approaches, NMSI searches the land for already successful programs—those with quantifiable results— and scales them up nationwide. It has a number of initiatives, including a teacher-training program designed to improve instruction and align teachers on consistent Common Core-defined content. NMSI's

---

29. "100Kin10," 100kin10.org/page/funding

impressive Advanced Placement program aims to show that more students, especially from underrepresented groups, can pass A.P. courses in math and science. Operating in 462 schools in 18 states, the program combines extensive teacher training with higher-quality instructional materials plus financial incentives for teachers and students alike (bounties are paid for good scores). It has realized early success: The first six states to participate all finished in the top 10 nationally in their percentage increase of passing A.P. scores in math and science since 2008 (when the program started).[30]

Though NMSI is not aimed at high-potential students *per se*, it is helping elevate the overall level of American STEM education. A terrific byproduct of this lift-all-boats approach is that our top-achieving students will have access to more and improved STEM teachers making high demands in a friendly competitive learning culture. This is increasing opportunities to excel in schools that previously settled for much lower performance.

Advanced arts education

Despite the inclusion of visual and performing arts in the federal definition and some state definitions of giftedness, the majority of programming for high-potential students focuses on those who show promise in standard academic fields. One reason is because identifying artistically gifted youth is a subjective undertaking. Standardized assessments of art-related talents simply do not exist in the same fashion that assessments of reading, writing, and math do.

This is not to say that assessing potential in the arts is impossible. There are art-related A.P. exams, for example. There are also certain commonly recognized indicators of skill in many of the arts. These vary widely in acceptance and universality, though, and fields like music are very different from painting, never mind dance.

Some educators believe that providing artistically gifted students with high-level programming is as important as challenging other gifted students. The National Research Center on the Gifted and Talented calls for bringing together students "with high interests and abilities in art in ways that will broaden and deepen their knowledge about art, sharpen their art skills, and offer them learning opportunities rarely found in a

---

30. National Math + Science Initiative, About Us, nms.org/AboutNMSI.aspx

regular art classroom setting."[31] But while evidence exists on the benefits of arts education in general (discussed below), there is little research on successful instruction of artistically talented students.[32] In the visual arts in particular, few studies and no large-scale investigations exist evaluating the effectiveness of gifted-student programming.[33]

Philanthropists with a particular interest in developing serious artistic talent in students might support research on the effectiveness of ability grouping or acceleration as related to artistically talented students. They might fund rigorous evaluations of existing programs. They might study the demographics of intensive art education. They could establish or support partnerships between arts-related institutions like symphonies or museums and schools. They make successful programs available to more boys and girls[34] Following is some information that could aid such efforts.

The Arts Education Partnership is a national coalition of more than 100 education, arts, business, cultural, government, and philanthropic organizations that was established jointly by the U.S. Department of Education and the National Endowment for the Arts. Its goal is to secure a high-quality arts education for every American student. It attempts to accomplish this by making strong programs more accessible, improving arts-education practice, and researching how arts education strengthens K-12 education more broadly. It provides partner organizations with access to recent findings, and encourages collaboration among participants.

The partnership's research clearinghouse, ArtsEdSearch.org, focuses on student outcomes associated with arts learning. It provides a bevy of findings on the value of arts education to student development. For instance, drama programs contribute to literacy and language development; studying music can improve math skills, including raising SAT scores. Research suggests that low-income, minority, and English-deficient students improve their overall academic achievement when they are able to participate in the arts.[35]

Another partnership offering is its State Policy Database, funded by the Hewlett Foundation. Funders seeking specifics on the laws and regulations associated with arts education in their states will find this useful. It

31. Gilbert A. Clark and Enid Zimmerman, April 1994, "Programming Opportunities for Students Gifted and Talented in the Visual Arts," gifted.uconn.edu/nrcgt/reports/rbdm9402/rbdm9402.pdf

32. Ibid.

33. Ibid.

34. Ibid.

35. "ArtsEd Search," artsedsearch.org/students/research-overview

enables the user to generate state-level policy reports covering more than a dozen subjects. For example, a donor interested in California's policies would learn that the state has pre-K content standards for visual and performing arts, and requires arts instruction in elementary and middle schools; however, California does not require arts education assessments, or stipulate any arts requirement for high school graduation.[36]

A wide array of dedicated schools focus on high-level arts education. For example, Houston's High School for the Performing and Visual Arts, which was developed more than 40 years ago, evolved from a local realization that gifted young artists needed specialized, rigorous training if they were to be prepared for the intense competition they'd face in colleges, conservatories, and the professional arts world. The school requires the same academic curriculum and graduation requirements as all district high schools, but in addition students spend three hours every day studying one of the art disciplines. Students must audition for admission.[37]

St. Paul, Minnesota, has the High School for Recording Arts, a charter school now open for 15 years, which serves an almost entirely low-income and African-American student body. Though it has the same graduation requirements of other state high schools, students have access to recording studios and receive training related to careers in the recording industry. The school has numerous corporate sponsors, including State Farm Insurance.[38]

Philadelphia's High School for the Creative and Performing Arts, a district magnet school, provides students with a dual academic/arts college-prep program. It offers a program of study in six arts disciplines: creative writing, dance, drama, instrumental music, vocal music, and visual arts. To be accepted, students must meet academic requirements (GPA and test scores) and pass an audition in one of the six disciplines. *Philadelphia* magazine named it one of the dozen best schools in the city in 2012.

Many other cities, from New York to Miami, and Baltimore to Los Angeles, have established high-profile high schools to serve artistically gifted students. Few regions have more than one option, however, and many places have none. Interested funders might support such existing schools, or found new ones in their communities of interest, either through the district— potentially as a magnet program—or as a charter school.

---

36. "Arts Education Partnership," aep-arts.org/wp-content/DatabaseSupport/StatePolicyReportPopWindow.php

37. "The High School for the Performing and Visual Arts," houstonisd.org/hspvarts

38. "High School for Recording Arts," hsra.org/Friends-and-Partners.aspx

Technology-enhanced learning

For years, a debate has raged about how best to educate students of different ability levels. "Tracking" groups together students with others achieving at the same levels, enabling their teachers to deliver roughly the same content to an entire class. The downside was that those grouped together because of low achievement may have been provided with less-effective teachers and exposed to less demanding material. Even in the most effective schools, tracking is easily attacked on the old grounds of "unfairness" and "elitism," and such charges have indeed sometimes been leveled against efforts to match students to courses of study depending on their demonstrated abilities.

And so, tracking fell into bad odor in some places. Doing away with tracking and mixing kids of various achievement levels in every classroom may expose low-achieving students to higher-quality instruction. But if most of the teacher's time is dedicated to catching up those farthest behind, high-achieving kids can end up unchallenged, bored, and ultimately disengaged.

If high-potential children are not challenged, they can disengage. These students are a key to our future international competitiveness, job creation, and civic leadership. Squandering this natural resource is a price we cannot afford.

Nor should one forget the toll exacted on teachers asked to instruct students of widely varying abilities within a single class; their planning time swells and they can finish each class feeling that no one really got the attention deserved. When state and federal accountability systems started demanding over the last decade or so that every school's lowest-performing students be pulled up to minimum levels—backed by carrots and sticks—teachers and schools were forced to allocate their limited time and money. Institutional incentives for focusing on top-performing students withered away.

Today's conundrum is thus how to personalize instruction so each student receives an appropriate course of study—underachievers, middle-of-the-roaders, and top performers alike. Recently, technology has begun to offer a possible way out of this box. Online instruction blended combined with customized tutoring to fill the gaps discovered by computerized assessments shows great promise as a new way to make schooling more effective for learners of all speeds.

Blended learning

Between 2000 and 2009, the number of K-12 students taking at least one online course as part of their schooling grew from roughly 45,000 to more than three million.[39] When more recent data is made available, we're certain to see that number swell even more. Many young people have taken to computerized instruction, and we are so far only scratching the surface of its possibilities.

There is an enormous interest today among education reformers in techniques, programs, and schools that blend 1) online learning with 2) continual electronic skills assessment, and 3) targeted in-person instruction to fill knowledge gaps, as an alternative to traditional one-size-fits-all classroom lecturing. One of the non-profit groups leading research in this area, the Clayton Christensen Institute for Disruptive Innovation (formerly the Innosight Institute), believes that blended learning that melds those three elements has the potential to revolutionize K-12 education—especially for students at the bottom and top of the achievement spectrum who often get lost in the shuffle of homogenized group teaching in conventional classrooms.[40] "Personalizing learning, by tailoring students' learning experiences to their individual developmental needs, skills, and interests, is one promising approach to ensuring that all students—including gifted students—can reach their full potential," says Bill Tucker of the Bill & Melinda Gates Foundation.

Recently, The Philanthropy Roundtable published a detailed donor's guide, authored by Laura Vanderkam, focused entirely on the latest information available on blended learning. We strongly recommend that funders interested in this topic consult *Blended Learning: A Wise Giver's Guide to Supporting Tech-assisted Teaching*, which is available in a variety of printed and electronic forms through the "Guidebooks" section of PhilanthropyRoundtable.org. Given

39. innosightinstitute.org/innosight/wp-content/uploads/2011/01/The-Rise-of-K-12-Blended-Learning.pdf
40. Michael B. Horn and Heather Staker, January 2011, "The Rise of K-12 Blended Learning," innosightinstitute.org/innosight/wp-content/uploads/2011/01/The-Rise-of-K-12-Blended-Learning.pdf

that guide's comprehensiveness, we will only lightly discuss in this volume the potential of blended approaches to significantly boost gifted students.[41]

Online supplementation is "a natural way to get more educational offerings into the hands of students who otherwise wouldn't have access to certain courses or opportunities," notes Ray Ravaglia, associate dean and director of Stanford Pre-Collegiate Studies. Because of its powerful ability to customize the study courses of individual students, some educators prefer to call blended learning "optimized learning." Certainly it opens vast new worlds to high-potential students. "Online learning takes high-performing students and lets them excel," asserts Allison Powell of the International Association for K-12 Online Learning.[42] It's "not just integrating technology into the classroom," she notes, but relies on daily feedback on where each student is understanding the lessons and where he is not, "and using that to push individual students where they need to be pushed. It's using technology as a tool to get the data a teacher needs to ensure that kids are learning and being challenged."[43]

For this reason, one of blended learning's key constituencies is students "who want more variety or challenge," according to Vanderkam. The technique allows, for example, students in small or rural schools to have access to a wide array of A.P. courses. It lets schools offer children a longer menu of languages. It allows intellectually precocious kids to acquire college credits without leaving high school.

The Lovett & Ruth Peters Foundation has made major investments in blended learning programs precisely because they allow all kids to learn at their own pace. Challenging high-potential students is part of the appeal. Foundation president Dan Peters warns that "We ignore high-potential students at our peril. If they are not challenged, they can disengage and even drop out due to boredom. These students are a key to our future international competitiveness, job creation, and civic leadership. Squandering this natural resource is a price we cannot afford."

The broad umbrella of "blended learning" covers many program types and approaches to instruction. It can be instituted at the level of the district, school, classroom, or in individual instruction. It may incorporate online

41. Laura Vanderkam, *Blended Learning: A Wise Giver's Guide to Supporting Tech-assisted Teaching*, The Philanthropy Roundtable, 2013
42. Ibid.
43. Interview 5/16/13

content into a lesson, a single course, or an entire curriculum.[44] In any of these forms, blended learning has enormous potential to enhance the education of highly talented students. It "allows gifted students to seek their own level; they can move at their own pace without hitting the glass ceiling that often exists in traditional public schools," explains Elfi Sanderson of Northwestern University.[45]

Another advantage of blended learning, properly structured, is that it can allow teachers extra time to work with small groups or individual students on tasks personalized to meet each student's needs. That's good for every student. It is certainly welcome news for fast learners who may need to be engaged in more in-depth study than standard classes would afford. It can also lead to a wide array of different methods of study and assignments.

> Between 2000 and 2009, the number of K-12 students taking at least one online course as part of their schooling grew from roughly 45,000 to more than three million. Online learning has tremendous potential to enhance the schooling of quick learners.

Blended environments allow advanced students to move ahead on their own without putting demands on a teacher who may need to work at a slower pace with the rest of the class.

Philanthropists wanting to invest in blended learning have countless options. They can partner with local districts to pilot blended approaches. They can ensure that state policies and funding support such experimentation. They can invest in the non-profits and commercial firms developing the content that is delivered online. Vanderkam suggests scores of specific strategies, for donors of all interests and varying grant levels, in the *Blended Learning* guidebook.

One popular strategy for philanthropists who are already involved is investing in charter-school networks that are currently using blended approaches with good results. For instance, Rocketship Schools, founded

---

44. International Association for K-12 Online Learning, October 2011, "National Standards for Quality Online Courses," inacol.org/cms/wp-content/uploads/2012/09/iNACOL_CourseStandards_2011.pdf

45. Interview 5/20/13

in 2007 in San Jose, California, are now expanding to Milwaukee and other cities thanks to support from the Lynde and Harry Bradley Foundation.[46] Another charter network that is one of the national leaders on implementing blended learning, Carpe Diem Schools, got its start in Arizona, but is now planning expansions into Indiana, Ohio, Texas, and other states.[47] One aspect of Carpe Diem's model that potential donors may find attractive is that its schools are able to operate with less funding, leaving some surplus after state per-pupil reimbursements that can be invested in starting new schools, purchasing buildings, and other expansions that most charter schools have great difficulty financing.[48]

The Charter School Growth Fund, which counts among its donors the Lynde and Harry Bradley Foundation, Louis Calder Foundation, Daniels Fund, Doris & Donald Fisher Fund, Charles and Lynn Schusterman Family Foundation, Charles and Helen Schwab Foundation, Robertson Foundation, and William E. Simon Foundation, helps expand and replicate the best charter schools in America. They have a keen interest in the intersection of charter schooling and technology. Alex Hernandez, the CSGF partner leading the organization's investments in blended learning, suggests that "as personalized learning becomes more mainstream, we see opportunities to provide more individualized support for our highest-performing students, and all students for that matter."

Funders might also consider seeding and developing new blended models with particular promise for stimulating high-potential students. As with the school reform movement generally, the vast predominance of blended-learning energy is currently going into efforts to pull low-achieving kids up toward normal proficiency. Though more customized learning will by definition be helpful to high-achieving kids as well, very little attention has been directed on the particular problems and needs and challenges of high fliers, so there are opportunities to be a pioneer here.

The technology of individualized learning is still so new and unsettled that experts agree the field has yet to scratch the surface of possible approaches. Tom Vander Ark, author of *Getting Smart: How Digital Learning is Changing the World* and former education head at the Gates Foundation, argues that for

46. Laura Vanderkam, *Blended Learning: A Wise Giver's Guide to Supporting Tech-assisted Teaching,* The Philanthropy Roundtable, 2013

47. "Carpe Diem," carpediemmeridian.com/about

48. Laura Vanderkam, *Blended Learning: A Wise Giver's Guide to Supporting Tech-assisted Teaching,* The Philanthropy Roundtable, 2013

all the promise of the early blended learning experiments, proponents have only begun to explore potential variations.[49] For just one example, online learning could have tremendous potential to improve the schooling of the large number of gifted students living in rural areas.

While blended learning's novelty provides opportunities, it should also inspire some healthy caution. There is too much we don't know about its strengths, weaknesses, and long-term effects on student learning for anyone to treat it as a miracle cure. As a program officer from the Bill & Melinda Gates Foundation recently noted, "part of me is nervous that the dialogue and enthusiasm is outpacing the results."[50] Donors should steer clear of the many low-quality investments (like simply handing out laptops or iPads) that are promoted today as "high-tech" solutions. Givers intrigued by the possibilities but not wanting to overhype this new field may decide that funding research on the intersection of new technology and high-performing students is a prudent investment at this stage.

Supplemental online offerings

One of the best features of smart technology is that it can differentiate information for different individuals, thus personalizing learning. The Reasoning Mind (RM) is a non-profit organization dedicated to improving students' math skills by applying technology in much this customizing way. RM has created an online math program offering lessons and support tailored to each student's separate needs. Because RM was designed for use in either a classroom or homeschooling environment, students receive the dual benefits of uniquely tailored lessons plus face-to-face support from a teacher.[51]

Reasoning Mind works with a variety of schools—urban, rural, suburban, district, charter, magnet, and private alike. Homeschooled students can also enroll individually.[52] The courses are based on an international curriculum that has helped millions of students in Russia, China, and Singapore excel in mathematics.

Curriculum developers worked with expert mathematics teachers in Moscow to design the program's materials. The Russian curriculum, developed in the mid-20th century, was the foundation of the Chinese mathematics curriculum; the Chinese curriculum in turn served as the

---

49. Ibid.
50. Ibid.
51. "Reasoning Mind," reasoningmind.org
52. Ibid.

foundation for Singapore's much-lauded math curriculum. Today, most countries that perform at the top of international math assessments have a national curriculum that has grown out of the Russian program.[53]

RM offers three courses: Basic I, for students in second through fourth grades, touches on geometric, algebraic, and numerical concepts that will be covered in-depth in subsequent courses. Basic II was created to give students in grades four through five "a deep conceptual understanding of whole numbers, to begin their study of common fractions and decimals, and to develop an understanding of key geometric and algebraic notions."[54] Basic III, was developed for students in grades five and six, and provides students with an in-depth study of non-negative rational numbers, ratios and proportions, and basic algebraic transformations. The curriculum is designed and taught "in a connected, spiraling fashion…. Problem solving is the key learning activity," and "true conceptual understanding and intuitive command of mathematical ideas" create its foundation.[55]

RM provides in-depth training for teachers, as well. The "Reasoning Mind Qualification Course" is a two- or three-day undertaking that teachers go through the summer before they offer RM in a classroom. The course covers the student and teacher software, RM classroom strategies, and an introduction to the RM curriculum. The companion "Reasoning Mind Certification Course" includes up to 100 hours of study. Teachers work through it during their first year of teaching RM. It focuses on details of program content and teaching strategy.[56]

Students using RM have demonstrated improved results in their mathematics knowledge and skill as measured by various standardized tests. For example, after using RM for one year, below grade-level second and third graders in California were able to catch up to their grade level.[57] A randomized-control trial of fourth graders in East Baton Rouge Parish in Louisiana, completed in 2011, likewise demonstrated a clear improvement of math scores compared to students not using RM.[58] The Reasoning Mind has a long list of philanthropic supporters,

53. "Some Key Differences Between RM's Curriculum and Traditional Curricula Used in the United States," reasoningmind.org/pdf/Differences_Between_RM_and_Traditional_Curricula.pdf

54. "Reasoning Mind," reasoningmind.org

55. "Some Key Differences Between RM's Curriculum and Traditional Curricula Used in the United States," reasoningmind.org/pdf/Differences_Between_RM_and_Traditional_Curricula.pdf

56. "Reasoning Mind," reasoningmind.org

57. Ibid.

58. Ibid.

including the ExxonMobil Foundation, Cockrell Foundation, Hoglund Foundation, and Houston Endowment.[59]

Renzulli Learning, briefly discussed in Chapter 4, is another online program that aids personalized instruction of students. It individualizes lessons based on interests, learning preferences, and expression styles. Each student completes an online questionnaire that enables the software to create a personal profile.

The Renzulli database includes 40,000 online educational materials. The personal profile helps both students and teachers sort through these resources and mix and match the best, most appropriate supports for each learner. Teachers can also use the database to find classroom activities and materials that accomplish specific objectives or teach to particular standards.[60] The resources in the Renzulli Learning database are all vetted, and they place a strong emphasis on problem solving, creativity, and critical-thinking skills.

The university, non-profit, and commercial programs sketched above are just a fraction of the online resources now available for educational enrichment of students who may need more than what their local school is offering. Using the examples above as guides to the type of options available, donors might support high-performing students in a variety of ways using technology. For instance, philanthropists could engage local colleges and universities to develop initiatives like those above. They might encourage local districts and schools to publicize these offerings to high-capacity students, and help them fold them into the school year. Donors can help developers bring additional products like these to fruit, and to the wider U.S. market.

The academic aids available to high-flying kids are growing in number and quality. Matching children to supplements that can challenge them, and removing roadblocks to school collaboration in this process, so parents and students don't have to navigate these options alone, are important tasks. The goals for funders should be to help expand the supply of offerings available, help expand the demand for such offerings among high-potential kids, and ensure that students and supports get properly matched, and with support, not resistance, from local educators.

A word about online quality
There's no doubt that the K-12 world is currently excited by the possi-

---

59. Ibid.

60. "Renzulli Learning," renzullilearning.com

bilities for online and blended learning. Whether this is a passing infatuation or the next stage in our ongoing evolution from factory-style to individualized education remains to be seen. Whether these new tools actually bring clear enhancement of student learning will determine that.

There are those who believe these new technologies will not have climactic effects on the educational experiences of our most gifted kids, or of other students. In a 2010 *Slate* article, journalist Amanda Ripley sought to determine what high-performing schools around the world looked like. Her conclusion: "Classrooms in countries with the highest-performing students contain very little tech wizardry, generally speaking. They look, in fact, a lot like American ones— circa 1989 or 1959. Children sit at rows of desks staring up at a teacher who stands in front of a well-worn chalkboard."[61]

> An average U.S. high school offers eight A.P. courses; Northwestern University offers 24 on line. "It's a matter of access for kids. They come from all over the country."

During our tour of the BASIS school in Washington, D.C., we were surprised by the lack of classroom technology throughout the building. Every class we visited looked a lot like that 1989 or 1959 classroom described by Ripley. BASIS is living proof that academic success today doesn't *have to* involve tech wizardry.

Whether online tools ultimately become dramatic disruptors or forgettable fads will ultimately depend on the quality of their conception and the precision of their use. On the first score, most of the experts with whom we spoke strongly advised that donors familiarize themselves with the quality standards for online learning developed by the national online learning association iNACOL. Ms. Sanderson of Northwestern's Gifted Learning Links recommends that donors look closely at any course syllabi to determine the level of instruction taking place. "It's not just about the technology; look underneath the bells and whistles to ensure that the content is taught in such a way as to require higher-level critical-thinking skills."

---

61. Amanda Ripley, "Brilliance in a Box: What do the best classrooms in the world look like?" *Slate*, October 20, 2010, slate.com/articles/news_and_politics/the_hive/2010/10/brilliance_in_a_box.html

Another aspect of quality is useability. In order to practice blended learning successfully, teachers must be given accurate, timely reports summarizing the progress of students through their digital curriculum. That allows the instructor to quickly spot sticking points and holes in understanding, so she can swing into action to fill the gaps. This is partially a technology issue—is the system capable of collecting and analyzing data on the fly, and then producing useable information for the supervising? It is also a human-capital issue: teachers must be able to understand this feedback data and available to respond to it with classroom action, or else all the effort to individualize lessons will be mostly wasted.

New technologies can be seductive, but unless they are wielded expertly by properly recruited and prepared teachers, they can turn out to be useless. Or worse than useless if the old system of textbooks, lesson plans, classroom lectures, and so forth has been thrown out without a functional replacement. Even where the technological tools are excellent, very bright students, and also other students, will always require guidance from wise, experienced, rounded educators capable of helping them assemble a course of study that builds progressively and doesn't have blind spots.

For philanthropists this probably means heeding both the verb and the noun in the phrase "Proceed with Caution." By all means, embrace the enormous promise of customized instruction. But don't get swept up in fads, don't make the tools more important than the content, don't lose sight of the hard-won discoveries of generations of educators that all learning requires diligent application, perseverance even when the task is not fun, balance among competing wisdoms, respect for the discoveries of preceding generations, and so forth.

Dr. Ravaglia of Stanford urges donors to bring a "venture" mentality to their philanthropy in this area. Embrace experimental innovation while setting clear expectations for results. Establish targets, closely monitor outputs, and tie fund disbursements to delivered promises. "Be clear about expectations up front, and, if possible, structure gifts into segments that can be released as measurable progress is made. Donors need to have an active relationship with their recipients."

University courses

A number of universities like Stanford and Northwestern now offer online coursework for K-12 students. These supplement students' traditional high-school studies, providing high-achieving students with more specialized or challenging coursework than their schools are able to offer. These informal options are ideal for students who are highly motivated and self-directed (which of course does not cover all gifted students!).[62]

Gifted Learning Links at Northwestern University offers enrichment activities, honors classes, and A.P. courses for talented students in grades K-12.[63] To be eligible, students must either meet test-score requirements (at or above the 95th percentile) or complete an admissions portfolio that includes a report card, teacher recommendations, and student work samples.[64] Students from any part of the U.S. may partake. GLL offers a user-friendly course catalogue with class descriptions. The cost of tuition and fees typically comes to about $500 per course.[65]

Qualifying students can choose from a variety of courses. K-2 youngsters may partake of "Family Program" courses like *Math and Sports* or *Backyard Explorers*. Students in third through eighth grade are eligible for either "enrichment courses" that sprinkle in-depth knowledge of writing, math, technology, world languages, humanities, and science, or "core essential" classes that enable students to master essential subject-area content above their traditional grade levels.[66]

Students in grades three through twelve may choose independent studies tailored to a student's specific interest and competence. There are also extracurricular clubs for these ages, including architecture, robotics, and Model United Nations. Students in grades six through twelve are eligible for the High School Credit Program—which provides a variety of elective, honors, and A.P. courses that may not be offered at conventional high schools.[67]

According to Elfi Sanderson, the coordinator of the GLL program at Northwestern, it helps "gifted kids find what they're passionate about and what motivates them to learn." An average U.S. high school offers eight A.P. courses; Northwestern offers 24 online. "It's a matter of access for kids. They come from all over the country and the world. Some are home-schooled. Some live in rural areas or attend small high schools and don't have access to certain courses. We help fill that gap."[68]

62. "Learning Online: A Viable Alternative for Gifted and Talented Students," tip.duke.edu/node/624

63. "Gifted Learning Links," ctd.northwestern.edu/gll

64. Ibid.

65. Center for Talent Development, Family Program, Enrichment, & Core Essential, 2013-14 Course Catalogue, ctd.northwestern.edu/docs/ctd/GLL_2013-14_Enrichment_Catalog_FINAL.pdf

66. Gifted Learning Links: Individualized Online Courses for Gifted Students, ctd.northwestern.edu/docs/FRY%20Catalog%20GS%201213.pdf

67. Ibid.

68. Interview

GLL courses are all created in house by content experts. They put together the course and use technology and external tools to enhance the curriculum. One-to-one communication between teachers and students is available. In some cases, school districts partner with GLL and send small groups of students to take a high-level course that they don't offer. The cost of the tuition will often be cheaper for the district than hiring someone to teach one course for a small number of high-achieving students.[69]

During the 2012-13 school year, about 1,800 K-12 students were enrolled in GLL courses. Some schools will send one or more students at a time and pay for the course; others approve a course after a family's request but choose not pay for the instruction. Some accept neither the course nor the credit, and the student simply attaches the transcript to their college applications. Over the years, GLL has developed close working relationships with certain schools, districts, states and organizations, including the state of Ohio's iLearnOhio, the state of West Virginia,

> There are few initiatives that help gifted students who aren't minorities or in poverty match up with colleges that will stretch them.

the Pewaukee School District in Wisconsin, the Jack Kent Cooke Foundation, and the Next Generation Venture Fund.

Stanford University introduced its first online course for high school students (A.P. calculus) in 1990. From 1990-2006, the university continued to add courses for high-school students seeking advanced course work, on an à la carte basis. In 2006, the university substituted a whole-school solution, creating the Stanford Online High School.[70] School director Ray Ravaglia, explains that "we want to raise the quality of what is offered to students and to make sure that when they show up as undergraduates they are maximally prepared for challenging coursework and are ready to perform at their maximum potential."

Currently, the Stanford University Online High School serves students in 42 states and from 24 countries, across grades 7-12. Its structure makes the school a perfect fit for students who live in sparsely populated areas, who

69. Interview 5/20/2013
70. Interview 5/20/2013

must travel frequently, who are schooled at home, or who are precocious and ready for classes above their age level. At this online school, no one says you can only take senior-year classes when you reach age 17, and so forth.

The high school does more than just offer high-level courses. It links students to peers and teachers who understand their academic situation. "What makes gifted summer programs so successful is that a bunch of gifted kids who share a passion about a subject get to be in the same place, learning from a content expert. We wanted to capture that in our high school," says Ravaglia.[71]

The school takes a seminar-style approach to teaching and learning. All traditional lecturing and background information is pre-recorded and watched by students on their own time. Students also have traditional math problem sets and papers to write. On top of those elements come the school's unique seminars. These are interactive. Students participate in two video conferences each week, where they have exchanges with teachers and fellow students much as they would in a classroom seminar.

The high school also offers academic advisers, counseling for social and emotional development, and college counselors. Extracurricular activities are also part of the Stanford Online High School experience. There is a high school newspaper club, a yearbook club, and a culinary society (similar to an online version of the television show *Top Chef*). "We are trying to foster a dynamic community where students feel that they're in school together,"[72] says Ravaglia.

A key benefactor of the Stanford University Online High School has been John Malone (see Chapter 3 for his prior initiative in educating talented students, the Malone Scholars Program). The Malone Family Foundation funded the development and implementation of the Stanford high school in 2006, and then made a second investment in 2009 to enable the creation of a middle school. The foundation sees these online schools as an excellent way to reach high-potential students who live outside regions where there is a physical school granting Malone Scholarships, and a service to bright and motivated students more generally.[73]

Jumping right to higher-ed

Some high-powered students are ready for even more than these supplemental and distance-learning programs. A certain number may find that

---

71. Interview 5/20/2013

72. Interview 5/20/2013

73. Malone Family Foundation, malonefamilyfoundation.com/aboutfoundation_whoweare.html

early entrance into a full-time college-degree program is the right fit. Accelerated programs like the Early College Academy and the Program for the Exceptionally Gifted, both located at Mary Baldwin College in Virginia, provide students with accelerated access to higher education. The Early College Academy enables bright 16- and 17-year-olds to complete their high school degrees in tandem with college courses.[74] Students live on campus with other students and specially trained staff, and graze through a full college curriculum.

The Program for the Exceptionally Gifted serves students as young as 13 in a similar way. PEG students live in a special, fully supervised dormitory, and enroll full time in college classes. They are able to bypass some or all of their high school work and immediately pursue an undergraduate degree. "For many students," says director Stephanie Ferguson, "this is the first time they're in class with their true intellectual peers. They're part of a cohort with similar experiences, so they no longer feel out of place."[75]

Students entering PEG are generally not only intellectually advanced but also focused and self-motivated: "It's important to determine who's driving the process—the student or the parent. If it's the parent, the student may not be successful in this type of program. We try to tell them that. There's no one-size-fits-all model for gifted education. Our students do remarkably well in school and after graduation. But they have to want to be here, and to have the motivation to push through when things are tough. For many, this is the first time they experience a true challenge. They must learn how to study, how to ask for help, and how to advocate for themselves with their professors," explains Ferguson.

Currently, there are more than 70 students attending PEG from across the country and the world. Twelve similar early-college programs exist at other campuses across the nation like Bard College, the University of Iowa, and the University of Southern California, serving students as young as 13. The PEG application process is virtually identical to those of other selective postsecondary programs, requiring academic transcripts, recommendations, SAT or ACT scores, and interviews. The program charges the same amount as the college's standard student amount (tuition, room, and board totaling $37,120 for 2013-14), but it has a wide array of financial aid offerings from merit scholarships and need-based grants to a number of named scholarship programs and state-associated grant offerings.

---

74. Mary Baldwin College: Early College Academy, mbc.edu/early_college/eca
75. Interview 5/30/2013

Though the 13 programs are spread across the country, large regions, like the Southwest and the upper Midwest, lack one. For families with such youngsters, the prospect of sending their early- to mid-teens child off to a college hundreds of miles away may be prohibitive. Donors might think about working with other institutions of higher education to start similar programs. Philanthropic dollars could also be used to provide more scholarships at the 13 existing programs that welcome prodigies to campus early.

Matching high-achieving grads to demanding colleges

For personal and family reasons, most gifted students will arrive in college via the traditional path, after high school graduation. Some of them, though, don't ultimately land in places that will make the most of their talents. There are few formal efforts to ensure that academically talented students end up at selective colleges and universities that will pull their best capabilities out of them.

Mind you, many philanthropic programs exist specifically to get underprivileged students into top colleges. (A few of these were touched on in Chapter 3.) And top colleges themselves are eager to enroll racial and ethnic minorities and low-income students capable of higher-level academic work. They undertake elaborate admissions efforts and devote lots of financial aid to "balance" their classes with such students. Harvard University, for example, offers essentially a free college education to students whose families earn less than $40,000 a year.[76]

There are few initiatives, though, that help gifted students who aren't minorities or in poverty match up with colleges that will stretch them. Merit scholarships offered to students purely because they have shown special intellectual talents have mostly fallen out of fashion today (donors might think about re-creating some to encourage peak achievement). Instead, financial aid has come to be disbursed primarily according to financial need, often with little or no consideration to student achievement. High-flying students from poor households will qualify for bounteous college aid, and high fliers from wealthy families have lots of options. High fliers in between, however, often get pinched.

The result is that too many bright high-school graduates never enroll in colleges that can fully meet their academic abilities. When an academically strong student attends a college that is less demanding than her intellectual credentials would allow, researchers call that an "under-

---

76. Shankar Vedantam, "Elite Colleges Struggle to Recruit Smart, Low-Income Kids," NPR, January 9, 2013, npr.org/2013/01/09/168889785/elite-colleges-struggle-to-recruit-smart-low-income-kids

match." Studies show that academically undermatched students are less likely to graduate and then thrive in the labor market.[77]

The College Board estimates that nearly 41 percent of all the high school seniors who graduated in 2005 were undermatched at their college. Of those, 16 percent were *substantially* undermatched. This is often a loss to the student and her family. When it is a high flier whose wings are clipped, it is also a loss to the community and nation.

According to Stanford economist Caroline Hoxby and Harvard professor Christopher Avery, high-achieving low-income students who attend academically selective schools in large metropolitan areas (like Stuyvesant High School in New York City or Thomas Jefferson in northern Virginia) have close to 100 percent odds of attending an Ivy League or other highly selective college.[78] But high-achieving, low-income students from less famous high schools often end up in a college that doesn't demand as much as they are capable of. College undermatching of high-achievers from middle-income households is also quite common.

Almost by definition, high fliers are thinly dispersed across a wide geography, and those who attend a typical high school that doesn't offer much to gifted students may get lost in the shuffle, particularly if they don't come from a high-achieving family. Supporting efforts by highly selective colleges to disseminate information and recruit high-ability students across a wide geography of communities is a major gap that philanthropists could help fill. Dollars could be used to waive application fees for high achievers, to support aspirational mailings, to explain actual net costs to families not savvy about the tuition curve, to send staff to visit schools, to contact high school counselors, or hold information sessions. A recent study by Caroline Hoxby and Sarah Turner demonstrated that such basic efforts are not only quite effective at improving the match of precocious students to demanding colleges, but also inexpensive and easily copied.[79]

Donors willing to go beyond matchmaking assistance might actually underwrite the higher education of gifted students by establishing merit scholarships to reward and encourage high achievement. The major philanthropist Julian Robertson offered $24 million to

77. Jonathan Smith, Matea Pender, and Jessica Howell, "The Full Extent of Student-College Academic Undermatch," The College Board Advocacy & Policy Center, January 2012, aefpweb.org/sites/default/files/webform/Extent%20of%20Undermatch.pdf

78. Reported in Shankar Vedantam, "Elite Colleges Struggle to Recruit Smart, Low-Income Kids," NPR, January 9, 2013, npr.org/2013/01/09/168889785/elite-colleges-struggle-to-recruit-smart-low-income-kids

79. Ibid.

establish the Robertson Scholars Program at Duke University and University of North Carolina at Chapel Hill. The program places 18 top high school students at each university, and pays all of their college costs—tuition, all living expenses, a laptop computer, and full funding for three summers of travel, research, or internship. Houston businessman Robert C. McNair has donated $30 million to the University of South Carolina to draw in gifted students from out of state by offering them full scholarships, room and board, and other fees for four years, on the basis of academic merit and character. The Niswonger Foundation helps send talented students from 17 school districts in rural northeast Tennessee to the college of their choice. In return, the beneficiaries are asked to return to their home region to serve in their profession for at least one year for every year they are supported. Currently, 18 students are being funded.[80] Interested donors will find many opportunities to establish similar scholarships awarded directly on the basis of academic performance and promise.

---

80. The Robertson Scholars Leadership Program, robertsonscholars.org/index.php?type=static&source=2; The McNair Scholars program, sc.edu/ofsp/benefactors.html; The Niswonger Scholars program niswongerfoundation.org/about

▶ **Summary of Investment Possibilities**

- Support efforts to gather information on acceleration practices and advocate for wider acceptance and use of acceleration
- Invest in programs that offer more high-level STEM opportunities, including not only rigorous classes but also internships with universities and labs and rigorous after-school programs
- Invest in the growing movement to develop more effective STEM educators
- Support research into the artistically gifted, especially improved methods of identifying such students, and identify the most successful programs for nurturing them
- Help create new schools designed specifically to advance high-quality arts education
- Help expand and improve blended learning by advocating for smarter policies, acquiring the necessary technology, and producing high-quality content
- Support existing, or seed new, high-performing blended-learning charter schools
- Support research into how new technologies can best help high-potential children
- Disseminate information on the best supplemental online resources, and ensure that high-achieving students have access
- Work with institutions of higher education to develop high-quality online offerings, and make them widely accessible, especially to needy students
- Grow new early-admission programs at colleges and universities
- Fund scholarships at college early-admission programs for low-income gifted students
- Fund merit-based scholarships designed to match the highest-performing high school graduates with top-flight colleges
- Help elite universities identify and recruit high fliers

Finding Teachers Who Can Stimulate High Achievers

In 1983, *A Nation at Risk* warned that there were too few specialized teachers for the gifted and talented.[1] More than 30 years later, little has improved. In all of our interviews and research, possibly the most prominent message was that we must dramatically change how we recruit, train, develop, and retain teachers if we're to have any hope of better educating America's brightest children.

---

1. National Commission on Excellence in Education, *A Nation at Risk*, 1983, datacenter.spps.org/uploads/sotw_a_nation_at_risk_1983.pdf

Current state policies leave a gaping hole in this area. Very few teacher education programs offer any training at all designed to prepare graduates to work with high-ability students.[2] A majority of states require no special training for teachers assigned to specialized gifted and talented programs. And only a handful of states call for any annual professional development for professionals working in gifted education.[3] Only a minority of states even require districts to have any administrator for gifted children; just six of these require that administrator to have any training in gifted education; merely two states require a full-time administrator for gifted ed.[4]

Kate Walsh, executive director of the National Center on Teacher Quality, one of the nation's leading voices on educator effectiveness, offered this stark assessment: "If we want to produce more students capable of advanced work, we need to pay better attention to recruiting, training, and retaining

> All teachers should be content experts in the fields they are teaching. You can't do a good job teaching kids math unless you know and love math, nor English, nor history, nor science.

educators who are capable of teaching very fast learners." The National Center on Teacher Quality provides valuable research and advocacy that aims to pull the entire teaching profession up to higher quality levels. Their new handbook *Teacher Prep Review*, for instance, evaluates 1,100 colleges on how well they prepare their students to become K-12 educators.[5] Philanthropists who share this interest might consider partnering with the center on initiatives that aim to raise the teaching bar, and to cultivate a cadre within the profession who can meet the needs of high-potential children.

Today, not even our most lauded alternative programs for filling the teacher pipeline provide any specific training for stimulating top students. Teach for America doesn't. This was not part of the New Teacher Project. Funders may want to take notice of this gap.

---

2. National Association for Gifted Children, nagc.org/default.aspx

3. "2010-2011 State of the States: Summary of Findings," NAGC, nagc.org/uploadedFiles/Information_and_Resources/2010-11_state_of_states/Summary%20of%20Findings%20(final).pdf

4. Ibid.

5. Julie Greenberg, Arthur McKee, and Kate Walsh, *Teacher Prep Review*, National Council on Teacher Quality, June 2013

The result is that very few of America's existing educators are prepared to address the needs of gifted learners and ensure they reach their full potential. When placed in mixed-ability, heterogeneous classrooms with teachers untrained in gifted learning, high-capacity students generally end up drastically under-challenged and often disengaged—sometimes permanently.[6]

Experts stress that gifted students need to learn from teachers who are both experts in their content and trained to identify and cultivating abilities among top students. As one principal of a very high-performing selective-admissions school colorfully said, his district's teacher-assignment personnel have learned to send his school only "candidates who won't get eaten alive by our students."[7]

Yet, the research shows that teacher training is even weaker in practice than what the troubling state policies described above call for:

- In a national sample of teachers, 65 percent reported that their teacher preparation programs focused very little or not at all on how to teach academically advanced students.
- Of 7,300 randomly selected third- and fourth-grade teachers, 61 percent reported that they had *never* had any training in teaching gifted students.
- Evidence shows that most teachers give their high-achieving students little if any targeted attention, and rarely or never offer them different academic assignments.[8]

Because no national degrees or certification requirements exist for gifted educators, teacher training and ongoing professional development in this area varies wildly from place to place—usually around very low bare minimums.[9]

There is a skeleton professional apparatus in this area—29 states have at least one college with programming in gifted education. There are some undergraduate degrees, certain endorsement or certification pro-

6. NAGC, "Teacher Training: What the Research Says," nagc.org/uploadedFiles/Advocacy/Teacher%20 Training%20research.pdf

7. Chester E. Finn. and Jessica A. Hockett, *Exam Schools: Inside America's Most Selective Public High Schools*, Princeton University Press, 2012

8. NAGC, "Teacher Training: What the Research Says," nagc.org/uploadedFiles/Advocacy/Teacher%20 Training%20research.pdf

9. Duke TIP, "Teaching Gifted Children: National Guidelines and State Requirements," tip.duke.edu/ node/897

grams, some master's degrees, and even a few doctoral degrees paths that emphasize gifted education.[10] Few educators make this a specialty, or even a serious sideline, however. We need to better prepare some number of teachers who will work primarily or solely with the brightest students, while also training all teachers how to identify and nurture those with great capacity, and steer them to specialists who can meet their needs.

So long as many schools continue to resist the practice of grouping students by ability, today's conventional classrooms—25 kids of often sharply varying levels of ability—will be difficult places for both teachers and outlying kids. Educators will struggle to find a common denominator that suits only some of the pupils, and other-than-average students won't get the level of attention they need. The solution among special ed children over the last generation has been individualized instruction plans and personal teacher's aides who follows the needy student through heterogeneously grouped classrooms, all funded by large dedicated federal programs and state supplements. But students whose under-challenged minds are straining to move ahead get no specialized teachers to help them along their way.

If donors hope to enhance the educational opportunities of academically gifted youth, they will need to bolster the ranks of expert teachers with skills and inclination to meet the classroom needs of high-potential kids. This can be achieved in two ways: 1) By helping create high-quality programs at colleges (or outside of them) that will recruit and train teachers for this work. 2) By investing in continuing education offerings that improve the capabilities of existing educators in this area.

"We need a model," states Margaret Gayle, director of the American Association for Gifted Children at Duke University. If the existing neglectful system is going to be improved, it will be necessary "to change pre-service education, and simultaneously do professional development in a way that gives teachers the training they need to look at children differently and nurture their talents."[11]

Forming better teachers

Two of the leading advocates on this topic, the Council for Exceptional Children and the National Association for Gifted Children, have jointly developed ten standards for enhancing gifted-and-talented teacher education. These emphasize teacher knowledge base, a deep understanding of the needs of gifted children, research-based instructional strategies,

10. Ibid.
11. Interview

optimal learning environments, and the skills necessary to identify and assess high-potential students.[12] NAGC has located 86 colleges and universities nationwide that offer some coursework in gifted education.[13]

It is very much up for debate whether more credentialing is going to help with the shortage of teachers capable of getting the best out of high achievers. Recent studies have questioned the link between teacher credentials and teacher effectiveness.[14] New methods of data collection that link student achievement gains with individual teachers have enabled researchers to look more closely at the effectiveness of particular teachers and to identify qualities that make one more effective than another. As a result, we now know that little of the wide variation in teacher effectiveness is associated with traditional measures of training or licensing. Identifying high-performing teachers on the basis of credentials alone is impossible.[15]

So what factors *could* produce better teachers for our nation's top students? Schools like BASIS and Great Hearts focus on a teacher's content knowledge, rather than her certifications, as the crucial factor. "We look for content expertise first and foremost," explains BASIS donor Craig Barrett. "All teachers should be content experts in the fields they are teaching. You can't do a good job teaching kids math unless you know and love math, nor English, nor history, nor science." His BASIS colleague Michael Block concurs, "Our teachers are everything. They know and love their content, and everything flows from that."[16]

Philanthropist Bob Davidson agrees. "How can you guide a smart student through difficult information and answer her questions unless you are an expert? Teacher certificates and licenses don't matter much in this area."

There is evidence backing this approach. Researchers Dan Goldhaber and Dominic Brewer found that teachers who hold a degree in mathematics (as opposed to a general teaching degree) are associated with higher student math scores. Teachers with a bachelor's degree in a science subject are likewise associated with higher student test scores in science.[17]

12. NAGC, "Issues Addressed in the NAGC-CEC Teacher Preparation Standards in Gifted Education," nagc. org/index.aspx?id=1865

13. Hoagies' Gifted Education Page, hoagiesgifted.org/continuing_ed.htm

14. See Podgursky & Springer, 2010; Pelayo & Brewer, 2010; Goldhaber, Gross, & Player, 2010

15. Michael J. Podgursky and Matthew G. Springer, 2007, "Teacher Performance Pay: A Review," *Journal of Policy Analysis and Management*, Vol. 26, No. 4

16. Interview

17. Dan D. Goldhaber and Dominic J. Brewer, 1996, "Evaluating the Effect of Teacher Degree level on Educational Performance," *Developments in School Finance*. nces.ed.gov/pubs97/97535l.pdf

Getting content-expert teachers in front of bright kids seems a relatively straightforward task. Yet research shows that many schools do a poor job of recruiting teachers with degrees or experience in academic specialties. In many states, they aren't even allowed to hire mathematicians or people with literature degrees—policies require graduates of teaching schools, most of whose training is in classroom technique, not subject matter.

This is exacerbated by the low quality of many graduates of teacher colleges. A 2010 McKinsey & Company report pointed out that "school systems in Singapore, Finland, and Korea recruit 100 percent of their teachers from the top one-third of their academic cohort.... In the United States, about 23 percent of new teachers—and only 14 percent in high-poverty schools—come from the top one-third."[18] Top academic performers are both less likely to be recruited into the teaching profession in the U.S. and more likely to leave the profession in frustration if they do start teaching.

Relay Graduate School of Education
Given the sclerosis of many colleges of education and the state-level bodies charged with certifying teachers, building new institutions is one worthy place for donors to consider making a mark. The philanthropy-driven Relay Graduate School of Education recently established in New York City and subsequently other cities (profiled in *Philanthropy* magazine's Fall 2013 issue) is one exciting example of a new alternative way of minting more effective teachers. The two-year course of study was created by top administrators from three of the highest performing charter school networks in the country (KIPP, Uncommon Schools, and Achievement First), and $30 million of seed funding was supplied by donor Larry Robbins and a group of philanthropists from the Robin Hood Foundation.

Relay is a new, independent institution of higher education focused on training new teachers with proven, practical techniques they can apply immediately in classrooms. Professors are current or former K-12 teachers with strong track records of success with students. The institution utilizes video extensively, both to disseminate the methods of exemplary teachers and to capture graduate students on film so they can be critiqued by themselves and by experts. Relay was licensed by New

---

18. Byron Auguste, Paul Kihn, and Matt Miller, "Closing the talent gap: Attracting and retaining top graduates to a career in teaching," McKinsey & Company, September 2010, mckinseyonsociety.com/closing-the-talent-gap

York state in 2011 to operate as a new kind of teacher's college, the first new independent graduate school of education in more than 80 years to receive credentials from that state.

Before you are granted a master's degree from Relay you must demonstrate that your students have made at least a full year's worth of academic progress, on average, during the year you spend guiding them. Fully half of the program's total graduation credits are tied to measurable student outcomes. Relay has ambitious plans to grow beyond its current New York City beachhead. In 2013 the school was operating training programs in three cities—New York, Newark, and New Orleans—training about 850 teachers. They plan to open in Houston and Chicago in 2014, and then other campuses around the country after that.

> If we want to turn on the next generation
> of K-12 students, it's essential that
> we magnetize the most talented and
> promising college graduates to the teaching
> profession, and offer them an on-ramp and
> training that will bring out their very best.

"More than 40 percent high school graduates express interest in becoming teachers, but by the time they graduate from college only about 10 percent of them actually pursue the profession," notes Norman Atkins, co-founder of Relay. "If we want to turn on the next generation of K-12 students, it's essential that we magnetize the most talented and promising college graduates to the teaching profession, and offer them an on-ramp and training that will bring out their very best over the long haul."

In 2013 Relay added school executives to their list of trainees, but still with a practical emphasis on teaching. They launched a yearlong program to train principals, focusing particularly on how to offer instructional leadership in one's school. In the first year, 150 principals from around the country took part.

TNTP, EdFuel, Education Pioneers

Another source of new blood in teaching is TNTP, started in 1997 as The New Teacher Project but now rebranded simply by its acronym. TNTP helps urban districts improve the way they recruit, train, and hire new teachers. In 2000, through its teaching fellows and TNTP Academy programs, TNTP began preparing high-achieving recent college graduates without traditional education credentials to become highly effective teachers in high-need schools. Both the fellows programs and the academy are quite selective, and ensure that their graduates are well trained both in their disciplinary content and in educational pedagogy before they are placed in some of our country's neediest classrooms.

Schools in the poorest neighborhoods get the first pick of TNTP-qualified teachers. High-achieving students in these schools will benefit from instruction from men and women who were themselves high academic achievers, and who have undergone proven, outcome-oriented teacher training. And the TNTP criteria mean these instructors have the specific content knowledge needed to keep up with their students who are capable of accelerated learning.

"The No. 1 thing schools can do to unlock the potential of their students is to give them great teachers," Ariela Rozman, TNTP's CEO told us. "That's no less true for our most advanced students than for those who are struggling. If we can raise the overall caliber of instruction in our public schools, students of all levels will rise."

EdFuel, a new organization funded by the Walton Family Foundation, is also aiming to improve the talent level in education over the next decade. They aspire to draw into education smart workers from other industries. They'll help these sector-switchers develop their talents and maximize their chances of building long-term careers in schooling.

Education Pioneers, which celebrated its tenth anniversary in 2013, is another organization that pulls top thinkers into education, though mostly as managers rather than teachers in its case. The organization provides school districts and high-quality charter school chains with carefully chosen graduate students or young professionals with skills in areas like finance, law, human resources, curriculum design, marketing, or business strategy. These individuals serve full-year or summer fellowships solving the particular problems they have been assigned to. Education Pioneers encourages the alumni of these fellowships (1,600 individuals at present) to keep their hand in education on either a full-time or part-time basis as they continue their careers. The group aspires to bring 10,000 additional talented individuals into school improvement projects by 2023. "If you want to change the world, one strategy stands out above all others: Bet big on talented people," says CEO Scott Morgan.

With this philosophy, it's not surprising that Morgan likes the idea of philanthropists encouraging schools to do a better job of addressing their top students. He suggests that focusing more on serving gifted kids may actually be a savvy "strategy to ensure that all students (including gifted kids from low-income families) realize their full potential."

Helping existing teachers

Of course, while efforts are being made to attract new talent to teaching, it needs to be remembered that, for the near future, today's 3 million existing teachers will provide the bulk of instruction. If existing teachers are going to do a better job of engaging smart students, they will need help from specialized professional development sessions, and alternative certifiers that train teachers how to improve their instruction of fast learners. It would be beneficial if there were many more organizations like the following:

Confratute

So named because it is "part conference, part institute, with lots of fraternity mixed in," Confratute is hosted every year by the Neag Center for Gifted Education and Talent Development at the University of Connecticut. It's a weeklong summer professional development conference for teachers and administrators interested in gifted education. The conference focuses on the special needs of quick learners, and means of deepening their instruction.

Participants can choose from a variety of modules like curriculum development, utilizing technology with advanced learners, or teaching twice-exceptional learners (those with both a high IQ and special learning needs).[19] Educators have opportunities to learn from experts, as well as to share ideas and resources with other teachers of high-potential students. The cost for each teacher or principal participating is $1,350— which covers all instruction, food, and housing for the week.

Confratute was founded in 1977 by Joseph Renzulli, the University of Connecticut researcher of education for the gifted mentioned earlier in this book. The keys to its 36-year success, Renzulli says, are "our focus on differentiation of instruction, high-end learning, and enrichment teaching, plus the fact that everyone who teaches at Confratute is selected from the very best professionals who spend the majority of their time directly with schools, teachers, and kids."

---

19. 2013 Confratute Preliminary Schedule, gifted.uconn.edu/confratute/pdf/Confratute_Schedule.pdf

The Educators Guild
The Davidson Institute's Educators Guild is a free national service for teachers and other professionals committed to meeting the needs of highly talented students.[20] It is an online discussion group that enables participants to share their experiences, ideas, and recommendations, and to ask questions of each other. The Ed Guild newsletter contains information for teachers and administrators on the latest resources covering gifted-and-talented education. The guild also offers free consulting services to its members—including consultation on lesson plan ideas, ideas on how to differentiate work for students of varying abilities, and advocacy tools.[21]

There is also a library where teachers can access presentations on topics ranging from classroom accommodations for fast learners, to battling myths about gifted children. There are also books and articles helpful to educators, links to organizations that focus on gifted education, and information about state policies.

> Gifted children are just as much a high-need group of children as are students who lag the national norms.

Relay
The master's degree programs at the Relay Graduate School of Education, described above, are designed specifically so that working teachers can take them part time. More than 40 percent of Relay's coursework is delivered online, making the program even more manageable for educators while they are already employed in classrooms. Relay training in the various cities where they intend to operate can thus help existing teachers get better, even as it is drawing fresh talent into the profession.

Is it time for a Teach for America for high-potential students?
It's important that funders engage with mainline teacher colleges to improve their output of educators capable of teaching gifted students, whether new graduates or mid-career professionals developing their skills. A more dramatic priming of the pump may also be necessary, how-

20. Davidson Institute for Talent Development, Educators Guild, davidsongifted.org/edguild
21. Ibid.

ever. As Michael Block of BASIS Schools told us, "we realized that in order to get Finnish-level results, we had to recruit from selective colleges." Given today's crying need for a cadre of especially talented new educators focused on the high-performing students who have been taken for granted for many years, we would like to see the creation of some analogue to Teach for America that turns out teachers specially prepared to stretch the top students who will be so important to our nation's future health, prosperity, and international competitiveness.

A grand nationwide recruiting and training effort in the mold of TFA would be an ideal way to draw bright college graduates into serving the public good. Gifted children are just as much a high-need group of children as are students who lag the national norms. Their happiness and life course will vary depending on how effectively their education draws their best out of them. And there is also a collective stake. Whether these high-potential children develop into merely good thinkers and workers, or into the kind of thinkers and workers whose innovations can lift an entire society to new levels of health, safety, wealth, and happiness, will affect every one of us. These specialized teachers would thus render a direct service to lots of underserved kids while also providing a gift to the nation by maximizing the talents of children who might otherwise coast or wander at levels far below their creative potential.

These teachers would not be radically different from others; the main difference would need to be their content expertise. To guide high-potential students to maximum levels of performance, you must know the substance of your subject cold. While TFA corps members are drawn from the top ranks of some of America's most prestigious universities, they are mostly fresh college graduates who lack advanced degrees and professional experience. Therefore, additional training in one or more subjects might be necessary.

So far as we know, there is no effort underway along these lines. But the need and potential are both great. Some group of entrepreneurial philanthropists might consider pursuing this difficult but potentially transformative venture.

▶ **Summary of Investment Possibilities**

- Launch and support efforts by colleges of education and alterative certification routes to recruit more talented teachers into the profession
- Advocate for stronger public policies related to the certification and training of teachers of the gifted
- Encourage existing teacher training organizations to give attention to high-potential students
- Support existing or help launch new professional development activities aimed at teachers of gifted students
- Support the creation of a Teach For America analogue for gifted students

Research, Policy, and Advocacy

A concentrated public campaign raising awareness of how weak the educational offerings to America's top students are at present is much needed. Such a campaign would point out why this is unwise as public policy, unfair, and unnecessary. The goal would be to gradually change attitudes, practices, laws and regulations.

Our research for this project left us with the strong conviction that the education of our quickest learners is not only completely ignored by most education reformers, but also lacks the basic understandings that are needed to begin changing this dire situation. As Chester Finn puts it, "This field is troubled from top to bottom. There's been little research. Leaders shy away from providing good definitions of giftedness. We don't know how many kids we're talking about. Or how many are getting adequate service. There's no effective lobbying."

There are several reasons for the neglect of this issue, starting with the prevalent but misbegotten view that "those kids will be fine," that their native wit alone predetermines their success, that it would be "elitist" to accommodate their special needs and potentials. But it's also clear that the field's lack of clear definitions and the thinness of hard evidence are

States need to face some accountability, for the first time, for fully educating their high-performing students. Requiring that annual state education reports include rates of above-grade-level performance would be a good legislative start.

also part of the problem. Other educational hobbyhorses competing for dollars and attention often rely on straightforward claims and explanations. Aiming at the "low income" has been easy since the formula for determining eligibility for the federal meals program became the common yardstick. It was when legal definitions of "disability" were broadened that resources began pouring into that category.

The vast majority of the energy and resources directed at school enhancement today—both governmental and philanthropic—is triggered by low income (relying on familiar Title I or Pell Grant formulas) or by disability (under IDEA and other special education definitions). The particular needs of high-potential children are addressed only in a thin tissue of state and local policies, and there is nearly no Federal presence. Joe Williams, executive director of Democrats for Education Reform, sees a need to fix this. "If we are serious about helping every child reach his or her potential, then strong, sound ideas about serving gifted students have to be on the table," said Williams. "At DFER we are mostly focused on meet-ing the needs of low- income and minority students and addressing the domestic achievement gap, but we don't believe that serving those students should come at the expense of enabling our best and brightest to excel. Right now, our most gifted kids are getting their hats handed to them by their international peers. That gap needs to close as well."

How research could help

A focused research and advocacy agenda led by philanthropists could help spark improvement in this area. Funders willing to consider such work might partner with an education-related think tank to take up any number of specific topics. There are small institutes around the country that are focused on gifted education, most of them at universities; these could be helpful in suggesting avenues that might be fruitfully explored. One donor who has for some time been active in funding research on this topic at academic centers throughout the country is John Malone. The Malone Family Foundation has underwritten studies at, among oth-er places, the Education Program for Gifted Youth (Stanford University), the Program for the Exceptionally Gifted (Mary Baldwin College), and the Center for Talent Development (Northwestern University).

Few of the broader education-research groups are doing much of substance in this area, however, and getting the ship of gifted education ungrounded and back into the education-reform mainstream could be a public service. Few if any of the research and policy organizations based in D.C. have any specialty in gifted education. Until that is remedied, the training of high-potential children may get short shrift, given Washington's current importance in journalism, public advocacy work, and governance. A few Washington organizations have shown some interest in this subject, though, and might fairly easily be persuaded by a donor to become involved.

Similarly, a philanthropist might engage researchers at one or more of the universities that currently operate centers focused on high-achieving chil-dren—which includes private institutions like Duke and Northwestern and large public schools like Purdue and UConn. Kansas University's CLEOS lab is already working in this area. It conducts research on high-potential students and ways to help them develop using a "research-through-service" model. High-school students are given college and career counseling while participating in the center's research.

These student subjects are nominated for the CLEOS program by teachers or counselors, based on their high creative potential. Students undergo psychological assessments, group discussions, and one-on-one sessions with CLEOS counselors. The aim is to help participants flourish, while learning more about what makes such students tick.

One example of research coming out of CLEOS: a set of profiles that aims to help teachers identify and support especially creative and talented students.[1] Throughout a period of five years the researchers, working with counselors in schools across Kansas, used the profiles to identify students with special creative potential. Of the 500 students uncovered, a third had never previously been identified as gifted (largely because their grades were not above average).

"There's never been an efficient way to find adolescents who could benefit from a creative career," CLEOS director Barbara Kerr stated recently. "Very often the traits that feed their creativity, like openness to experience and impulsivity, get them in trouble," Kerr said. "Many of them say that they're only noticed in school when they're in trouble. Creative kids tend to be a particular type of outsider, admired by their small cadre of friends for their art or coding abilities, but avoided by many because of their eccentricities."[2]

Apart from existing university-based research centers, a wide array of individual scholars are pursuing work related to high-capacity students. Their work tends to focus on one specific aspect of this population, often related to gifted students from underserved populations. For instance, Marcia Gentry, Matthew Fugate, and Jiaxi Wu of Purdue University recently authored a paper with the leading title, "Gifted Native American Students—Overlooked and Underserved, A Long-Overdue Call for Research and Action."[3] They identified barriers that talented Native American children face, including social marginalization, remote location, poverty, and poor schools.

In response to this paper, the Jack Kent Cooke Foundation partnered with the Gifted Education Resource Institute at Purdue to launch a program that provides scholarships and travel costs for high-potential Native American students living on reservations in Arizona, South Dakota, and

1. Sarah D. Sparks, "Project Uses famous Profiles to Identify Gifted, Creative Students," *Education Week*, March 6, 2013, blogs.edweek.org/edweek/inside-school-research/2013/03/gifted_student_profiles_aid_identification.html

2. "Project Uses Famous Profiles to Identify Gifted, Creative Students," *Education Week—Inside School Research*, blogs.edweek.org/edweek/inside-school-research/2013/03/gifted_student_profiles_aid_identification.html

3. Marcia Gentry, Jizxi Wu, and C. Matthew Fugate, "Talented Native American Children and Youth: A Call for Recognition and Service," gerinari.weebly.com/research.html

Minnesota, so they can attend summer residential academic programs at Purdue.[4] This is an example of how smart research can quickly lead to results. A problem was uncovered, a solution was offered, an organization adopted the proposed strategy, a program was created, and now students are receiving services. Creative donors could shepherd numerous initiatives through this type of research and development process, ending with a successful, targeted intervention.

Public-policy advocacy

Even weak federal action on education of high-potential students would be a step up from what exists today. For years, the main—often only—federal activity was the Jacob Javits Gifted and Talented Students Education Program, passed in 1988.[5] This law did not support programs. Instead, its purpose was to focus "resources on identifying and serving students who are traditionally underrepresented in gifted and talented programs, particularly economically disadvantaged, limited-English proficient, and disabled students."[6]

The Javits program had three main components: a forum for research; grants to colleges and state and local education agencies to develop models for serving underrepresented students; and grants to states and school districts to enhance gifted programs.[7] Funded projects included research on methods for teaching gifted students, professional development for teachers and administrators involved in gifted and talented education, and technology to provide gifted students with higher-level coursework.[8] Funding for the Javits program ranged from a low of $3 million in 1995 to a high of $11 million in 2002. Then—apropos of the declining attention to this field—it was completely defunded in 2011.[9]

In 2013, Senators Grassley (R-IA), Mikulski (D-MD), and Casey (D-PA) introduced a bill (the so-called TALENT Act) that aims to fold a bit of support for high-ability students into the massive ESEA law that governs Federal involvement in K-12 education.[10] This legislation professes four pri-

4. Ibid.

5. NAGC, "Jacob Javits Gifted and Talented Students Education Act," nagc.org/index.aspx?id=572

6. Ibid.

7. Ibid.

8. U.S. Department of Education, "Jacob K. Javits Gifted and Talented Students Education Program," www2.ed.gov/programs/javits/index.html

9. NAGC, "Jacob Javits Gifted and Talented Students Act: Annual Funding History," nagc.org/index.aspx?id=1006

10. The Association for the Gifted, cectag.org

orities: Supporting teacher development that aids the academic growth of high-ability students, addressing the excellence gap that imperils U.S. competitiveness, providing clearer data on student achievement, and bolstering best practices in gifted education.[11]

The bill would require a number of fundamental changes to the way states and districts identify and serve gifted students.

- States would for the first time face some accountability for educating the high-performing students—via a requirement that rates of above-grade-level student performance be reported on state report cards.
- States would have to expand professional development opportunities for teachers in gifted education.
- There would be a grant program for conducting research to improve and develop high-quality instructional practices.
- States would be required to create plans to identify and serve minority and rural students.[12]

The bill would not create any new programs; instead, it inserts gifted students as a new category into relevant areas of ESEA. This would, for example, require states and districts to outline in the hefty plans they already file to get Title I funding any steps they will take to support gifted students.[13] Whatever this bill's eventual fate, it at least represents progress in ending the political bowdlerizing that has written high-potential children out of the national education conversation in recent decades. Funder's considering federal advocacy should pick up some of its innovations.

Rather than pushing for a new dedicated program for talented youth like the Javits approach, philanthropists might want to encourage the alternative presented in the TALENT Act: embed gifted education in programs across the board. This would take many forms. The next reauthorization of ESEA, for instance, should require measurement and accountability not just for the number of students who meet minimum "proficiency," but also for the number who reach an "advanced" level. Charter schools focused on high-potential children should be named

11. The Council for Exceptional Children, "TALENT Act Charts New Course for Gifted, High-Ability Students," policyinsider.org/2013/03/talent-act-charts-new-course-for-gifted-high-ability-students.html

12. Nirvi Shah, "Updated: Bipartisan TALENT Act Puts Spotlight on Gifted Students," *Education Week*, April 15, 2011, blogs.edweek.org/edweek/speced/2011/04/bipartisan_talent_act_would_bo.html

13. The Association for the Gifted, cectag.org

as one of the priorities of the Federal Charter Schools Program. Tidbits related to educating high achievers should be embedded into the Title II supplemental education program, into the Teacher Incentive Fund, and so forth.

One big idea would be to advocate for a new addition to the Race to the Top suite of competitions: one focused on high achievers. The first competitions encouraged states to pursue four broad reforms. Those were followed by competitions seeking to advance early learning. Then district competitions for personalized learning. Why not one to encourage states to adopt policies and programs that would aid high-potential children?

The same "embed gifted throughout" strategy should be pursued in advocacy campaigns conducted in the separate states (which will always be where the bulk of U.S. education policy is established). In addition to fanning fresh interest in better educating high-potential students, donors should try to ensure that they are included in all

> Leaders in other countries aren't feeling sorry for the United States and our education struggles. We need to step up to the plate and address this challenge so we can compete.

existing programs and new initiatives at the state or local level to improve education. If a state is starting some new effort, or applying for a waiver from some current regulation, watchdogs should insist that provisions aiding gifted students be included. Every state will be working on a Common Core implementation plan in the near future. This is an opening to make certain there are strands dedicated to the schooling of high achievers.

Another productive area in which to act may be teacher evaluation systems—which states have been modifying dramatically over the last few years, and will continue to adjust in the years to come. Education reformer Jon Schnur recommended in an interview that states make sure that the rubrics covering classroom observations include indicators of whether educators are able to identify gifted students and differentiate instruction so that their needs are being met along with other students.[14]

Donors may find they have the highest leverage within today's accountability systems, which touch all schools, after spreading widely during the No Child Left Behind years. Given the unsettled nature of ESEA reauthorization (which has been overdue since 2007, with promiscuous granting of waivers being the only way the system has remained somewhat afloat amidst the stalemate in Washington), today is an ideal time to introduce into the national education debate arguments for ending the neglect of high-potential students by most schools and districts. This could be both a state and Federal push.

For example, when ESEA is eventually reauthorized, provisions could be added rewarding schools for moving students from proficient to advanced. Schools should be required to monitor and report on the performance of their highest performers, just as they do on their lagging performers. States should be encouraged to develop programs that allow their highest potential high school students to graduate early, or to dual enroll in high school and college courses during their latter years.

"If we are truly serious about providing excellence in education for all students," writes researcher Robert Theaker and colleagues, "then we should consider changing accountability systems to place emphasis on the growth of low-, middle-, and high-achieving students alike." Among other things, adding measures of changing results at top levels of achievement to the last decade's obsession with performance at the bottom would "subject some wealthy, underperforming suburban schools to fair and welcome scrutiny."[15]

There are some timely, technical aspects of this that funders need to keep in mind as they consider advocacy agendas. For example, one problem with most state tests today is that they are unable to accurately assess students at the very highest levels of performance—the tests effectively run out of room at the top. Laura Vanderkam, a contributor to the Davidson's book on gifted students, *Genius Denied*, notes in an interview that avoiding these artificial ceilings on tests is important if high-potential students are to be accurately identified, and any useful determination made on just how advanced they are.[16]

---

14. Interview, Jon Schnur, April 25, 2013

15. Robert Theaker, Yun Xiang, Michael Dahlin, John Cronin, and Sarah Durant, "Do High Flyers Maintain Their Altitude? Performance Trends of Top Students," 2011., edexcellence.net/publications/high-flyers.html

16. Interview, Laura Vanderkam, January 17, 2013

The fact that states are currently in the process of adopting fresh tests that will measure their success at meeting new Common Core standards makes this subject especially timely.

Jon Schnur also believes that test-related decisions being made soon will have an important bearing on future gifted education. In our interview, he underscored that for the next generation of tests "we need to make sure the bar for 'advanced' achievement is set high, and that this category gets visibility—instead of having all conversations focus on mere 'proficiency.'"

Countless education reform advocacy organizations already exist. Few if any, though, push priorities related to gifted education. While numerous state-based groups have fought for things like new curricular standards, tougher tenure rules, and expanded charter laws, efforts for high-potential kids were nowhere to be seen.

Funders could work with existing advocacy groups—for example, those pushing teacher effectiveness, charter schools, and school choice—to make sure they include better performance at the peak of the achievement spectrum among their priorities in some way. Funders should also work directly with advocacy organizations that specialize in high-flying students to create a campaign and agenda. Entrepreneurial donors may even choose to seed across the educational landscape brand new organizations devoted to this crucial issue.

A good yardstick could do wonders

One place where energetic donor advocacy holds special promise is in pushing for use of the Test for Schools (also known as the OECD Test for Schools). Based on the international standard PISA test, wide adoption of this annual exam would enable Americans to make accurate school-by-school comparisons of one institution to another, useful state-to-state comparisons, and even comparisons of U.S. overall performance to that of other countries. Hard data of this sort could blow away a lot of wishful thinking and mistaken complacency. As Jim Rahn of the Kern Family Foundation notes, "leaders in other countries aren't feeling sorry for the United States and our education struggles. We need to step up to the plate and address this challenge so we can compete."

These tests have been piloted and are ready for widespread use. A joint project of the Organisation for Economic Co-operation and Development and America Achieves—a national non-profit funded by, among others, Bloomberg Philanthropies, the Edna McConnell Clark Foundation, and the George Kaiser Family Foundation—the tests focus on reading, math, and science, and are geared for use "by schools and networks of schools to support research, benchmarking, and school improvement efforts."[17]

It could be very much within the influence of a determined philanthropist to get the OECD Test for Schools used in his state, local school districts, and particular schools. Widespread use of this assessment tool could be an important step toward improving the education of all students and thus setting ourselves up to be true competitors in a global economy.

Based on pilot administrations of the test, the results can be quite surprising, and may stun some educators. There are other schools that are impressively punching way above their weight class. The Newark-based branch of the superb Uncommon Schools charter network actually outperformed the national averages of some of the world's best-performing nations in a recent trial test, even though North Star serves an overwhelmingly low-income, minority student body.[18] One BASIS charter school outperformed the average of every country in the world in reading, math, and science.[19]

Then there's the other side of the coin: lots of schools that currently seem to be "good"—partly because the raw material coming in the front door includes lots of bright students—yet actually are not very effective at pushing students higher up the achievement ladder from where they began. In Shanghai, the OECD Test for Schools pilot showed, even the lowest-income students outperformed the wealthiest students in the United States.[20]

We have miles to go.

---

17. OECD, "PISA-Based Test for Schools," oecd.org/pisa/pisa-basedtestforschools

18. "Newark School Shows the World: Opinion," *The Star-Ledger,* blog.nj.com/njv_guest_blog/2013/04/newark_school_shows_the_world.html

19. Friedman, Thomas L., "My Little (Global) School," *New York Times,* April 2, 2013, nytimes.com/2013/04/03/opinion/friedman-my-little-global-school.html.

20. "Newark School Shows the World: Opinion," *The Star-Ledger,* blog.nj.com/njv_guest_blog/2013/04/newark_school_shows_the_world.html

▶ Summary of Investment Possibilities

- Fund research on gifted education at think tanks or universities to generate ideas for new policies and practices
- Fund some compelling tests: Turn a concept floated by a researcher or advocate into a living, breathing initiative
- Provide support to existing education advocacy groups if they add gifted-education issues to their agendas
- Support existing organizations that advocate for high-potential students, or sponsor the creation of new ones
- Seek to embed consideration of high-flying students in as many current and future education programs as possible
- Advocate for a Race to the Top program (or a state-level version) for high-potential students
- Provide funding so that schools, districts, or entire states can participate in the international "OECD Test for Schools," which can help document the scope of our international inadequacies, and whether and where we are improving

CONCLUSION

The glass-half-empty conclusion about the state of gifted education in the U.S. today is that we are woefully incoherent, inconsistent, and incomplete in what we offer our most capable students. The glass-half-full view is that there are plenty of examples of success to build upon, and wide-open fields for future angels to put their marks on. Truly, we have nowhere to go but up.

Given the messy state of the field, the many opportunities, and the lack of dominant voices, funders will have great leeway in deciding where and how to give. But studying the terrain is necessary. What is true in one community or state will be very different in another. Examine your target schools, districts, and states carefully before acting.

As they shift into action, philanthropists will have a wide range of alternatives available to them. We've already discussed many options throughout this volume. Building off-campus enrichment programs.

> There are plenty of examples of success to build upon, and wide-open fields for future philanthropic angels to put their marks on. Truly, we have nowhere to go but up.

Supporting in-school interventions. Promoting online and blended learning that lets students progress at their natural paces. Creating entirely new schools. Expanding successful ones. Enhancing the training of educators. Attracting new subject experts into teaching as a profession.

However you invest, you will have the chance in this overlooked corner of our education system to change countless lives. These will include the boys and girls you touch directly (for all children, including those who've been blessed with special abilities, have needs and vulnerabilities that schools must meet if the youngster is to flourish). And, later, there will be the reward of discoveries and creations by high fliers who were lifted by their access to the right kinds of schooling from *good* performance into society-changing *greatness*.

In the words of Jim Rahn of the Kern Family Foundation, the aim in pushing for less mediocrity in educating our top achievers "is not to shame teachers or principals; it's about ensuring that *all* students receive a world-class education. It's just as immoral to inadequately prepare a middle-class student as it is to academically shortchange a student in the inner city. The freedoms and economic prosperity we enjoy today are an inheritance that our generation must steward and pass down. The realities of globalization will require new, innovative strategies lest we leave things in worse shape for the next generation. We're in a global race; we need to draw out the best from all students, or we will have squandered our moment."

INDEX

ABOUT THE PHILANTHROPY ROUNDTABLE

The Philanthropy Roundtable is America's leading network of charitable donors working to strengthen our free society, uphold donor intent, and protect the freedom to give. Our members include individual philanthropists, families, corporations, and private foundations.

Mission

The Philanthropy Roundtable's mission is to foster excellence in philanthropy, to protect philanthropic freedom, to assist donors in achieving their philanthropic intent, and to help donors advance liberty, opportunity, and personal responsibility in America and abroad.

Principles

- Philanthropic freedom is essential to a free society.
- A vibrant private sector generates the wealth that makes philanthropy possible.
- Voluntary private action offers solutions for many of society's most pressing challenges.
- Excellence in philanthropy is measured by results, not by good intentions.
- A respect for donor intent is essential to long-term philanthropic success.

Services

World-class Conferences

The Philanthropy Roundtable connects you with other savvy donors. Held across the nation throughout the year, our meetings assemble grantmakers and experts to develop strategies and solutions for local, state, and national giving. You will hear from innovators in K–12 education, economic opportunity, higher education, national security, and other fields. Our Annual Meeting is the Roundtable's flagship event, gathering the nation's most public-spirited and influential philanthropists for debates, how-to sessions, and discussions on the best ways for private individuals to achieve powerful results through their giving. The Annual Meeting is a stimulating and enjoyable way to meet principled donors seeking the breakthroughs that can solve our nation's greatest challenges.

Breakthrough Groups

Our Breakthrough Groups—focused program areas—build a critical mass of donors around a topic where dramatic results are within reach. Breakthrough Groups become a springboard to help donors achieve lasting results with their philanthropy. Our specialized staff assist grantmakers committed to making careful investments. The Roundtable's K–12 education program is our largest and longest-running Breakthrough Group. This network helps donors zero in on the most promising school reforms. We are the industry-leading convener for philanthropists seeking systemic improvements through competition and parental choice, administrative freedom and accountability, student-centered technology, enhanced teaching and school leadership, and high standards and expectations for students of all backgrounds. We foster productive collaboration among donors of varied ideological perspectives who are united by a devotion to educational excellence.

A Powerful Voice

The Roundtable's public-policy project, the Alliance for Charitable Reform (ACR), works to advance the principles and preserve the rights of private giving. ACR educates legislators and policymakers about the central role of charitable giving in American life and the crucial importance of protecting philanthropic freedom—the ability of individuals and private organizations to determine how and where to direct their charitable assets. Active in Washington, D.C., and in the states, ACR protects charitable giving, defends the diversity of charitable causes, and battles intrusive government regulation. We believe that our nation's capacity for private initiative to address problems must not be burdened with costly or crippling constraints.

Protection of Donor Interests

The Philanthropy Roundtable is the leading force in American philanthropy to protect donor intent. Generous givers want assurance that their money will be used for the specific charitable aims and purposes they believe in, not redirected to some other agenda. Unfortunately, donor intent is usually violated in increments, as foundation staff and trustees neglect or misconstrue the founder's values and drift into other purposes. Through education, practical guidance, legislative action, and individual consultation, The Philanthropy Roundtable is active in guarding donor intent. We are happy to advise you on steps you can take to ensure that your mission and goals are protected.

Must-read Publications

Philanthropy, the Roundtable's quarterly magazine, is packed with beautifully written real-life stories. It offers practical examples, inspiration, detailed information, history, and clear guidance on the differences between giving that is great and giving that disappoints. We also publish a series of guidebooks which provide detailed information on the very best ways to be effective in particular aspects of philanthropy. These guidebooks are compact, brisk, and readable. Most focus on one particular area of giving—for instance, Catholic schools, support for veterans, anti-poverty programs, environmental projects, and technology in education. Real-life examples, hard numbers, management experiences of other donors, recent history, and policy guidance are presented to inform and inspire savvy donors.

Join the Roundtable Today

When working with The Philanthropy Roundtable, members are better equipped to achieve long-lasting success with their charitable giving. Your membership with the Roundtable will make you part of a potent network that understands philanthropy and strengthens our free society. Philanthropy Roundtable members range from Forbes 400 individuals and the largest American foundations to small family foundations and donors just beginning their charitable careers. Our members include:

- Individuals and families
- Private foundations
- Community foundations
- Eligible donor advisers
- Corporate giving programs
- Charities which devote more than half of their budget to external grants

Philanthropists who contribute at least $50,000 annually to charitable causes are eligible to become members and register for most Roundtable programs. Roundtable events provide you with a solicitation-free environment.

For more information on The Philanthropy Roundtable or to learn about our individual program areas, please call (202) 822-8333 or e-mail main@PhilanthropyRoundtable.org.

ABOUT THE AUTHOR

Andy Smarick is a partner at Bellwether Education, a non-profit working to improve educational outcomes for low-income students. He previously served as deputy commissioner of education for the state of New Jersey, and as deputy assistant secretary at the U.S. Department of Education. During a stint as a White House Fellow, he drafted a report on urban Catholic and other faith-based schools, entitled *Preserving a Critical National Asset*. In 2012 his book *The Urban School System of the Future* was published. Earlier in his career, Andy helped launch a college-prep charter school in Annapolis, Maryland, for underserved boys and girls. His articles on education have appeared in the *Washington Post, Baltimore Sun, Boston Globe, Education Next, National Affairs, Philanthropy*, and other publications.